A TRIP INTO THE MOMENT

Michael Huber

Copyright © *Michael Huber*, 2025

All Rights Reserved

This book is subject to the condition that no part of this book is to be reproduced, transmitted in any form or means; electronic or mechanical, stored in a retrieval system, photocopied, recorded, scanned, or otherwise. Any of these actions require the proper written permission of the author.

Table of Contents

Acknowledgments 1
Foreword 2
Preface 3
The Motorcycle Stories 5
   My First Motorcycle Arrest 6
   Romanian Roaming 1: The Transfagarasan Highway 10
   Romanian Roaming 2: The Transalpina Highway 13
   Vietnam: Charlie Don't Wheelie 16
   Zooming Through New Zealand 34
   India: Prelude to Adventure 47
   India: Rolling South 54
   India: Rolling North 62
   India: Amritsar 69
   India: Amritsar to Rishikesh 75
Travel Stories 78
   Racing the Sun 79
   Toad Rock Campground, British Columbia 81
   Charlie Don't Paddleboard: A Baja New Year's Story 84
   Paddle Boarding Horseshoe Bend 88
   Wildlife in the Southwest: Javelina 93
   Me for VP 95
   Mount Rainier 98
   El Condor Comida 101
   Baja in the Slow Lane 103
   A Whale of a (Baja) Tale 107
   Let my Turtles Go! 111
   The Legendary Fung Wah Bus 113
   Cuba Bound 115
   Outriding the Pandemic 118
   Tongariro Crossing, Tongariro National Park, New Zealand 131
   Memorial Day 133

Ayers Rock 1: Coober Pedy 135
Ayers Rock 2: The Great Ocean Road 137
Ayers Rock 3: Arrival 139
Cambodia 142
The Working from "Home" Years 145
Becoming a Digital Nomad: Testing the Waters 146
Life as a Digital Nomad: Exiting the Wheel 149
Nicaragua 152
Panama 155
Ecuador 158
Peru 164
Peru 2 (Machu Picchu) 168
Peru 3 (Lake Titicaca) 172
Peru 4 (It's Probably Time to Head Back) 175
Victoria, British Columbia 179
Returning to the USA 182
Digital Nomad: The Seattle Years 184
The Ride 187
Psychedelic Adventures 194
Ketamine 195
LSD 198
A Season of Change (Ayahuasca) 203
San Pedro (Huachuma) 213
Mushrooms (Psilocybin) 217
Scuba Stories 221
Scuba Certification 222
Indonesia 228
Koh Tao, Thailand 237
Rescue Diver Certification 239
Dos Ojos Cavern Dive – Mexico 241
Epilogue 244
About the Author 246
Biography 247

Acknowledgments

I want to thank my parents and sister for their support of my rather unconventional lifestyle over the past 52 years. Thanks go to Stephen J. Smith, my best friend and mentor for the past 30 years, to Lambykins, as my entertaining sidekick throughout these adventures, and to Joe Berk, for editing and helping my writing grow immensely over the past 8 years. I of course want to thank all the readers of these stories who may find some humor, life takeaways, sparks of motivation, and, most importantly, the knowledge of how not to do things. Thank you all!

Foreword

I was on a group ride in Baja with a bunch of people on adventure touring style motorcycles, and we had stopped to buy gasolina out of a bottle in Catavina, about 330 miles south of the border. There's not much down there except gobs of breathtaking scenery, and at the time, there certainly were no petrol stations. That's when I noticed it: A set of jump wings on the back of a tourbox, mounted on the rear of an adventure bike. Jump wings are a badge, a badge worn by those who completed the US Army's Airborne school in Fort Benning, Georgia. We had been on the road several days, and I was certain I knew everyone in the group. I was stunned, I didn't know that one of the group was, like me, Airborne.

I visually fixated on the jump wings, and then I looked at the rider standing next to the bike. He was smiling or laughing (I never did find out which) at my reaction. That's when I realized he wasn't with the group; he was coincidentally stopped for gas at the only place selling gas for over a hundred and fifty miles in any direction.

Mike Huber and I became friends almost immediately. We both had a US Army background, we both had served in Korea, we both loved motorcycles, we both loved Baja, and as I would learn, Mike also loved writing. One thing led to another, and Mike became a writer for an adventure blog I manage (www.exhaustnotes.us). With his world travels and flair for adventure, Mike was a natural on the ExNotes site.

As you read through these stories, you might wonder if Mike is hopelessly adrift and aimlessly wandering around the world. Don't fall into that trap. As J.R.R. Tolkien observed, not all who wander are lost.

- Joe Berk, July 2025

Preface

Written over the course of the past five years, this book details the incredible highs and crushing lows I experienced with my mental health. Death, at one point, was literally wound loosely in my inept hands. I understand we all have peaks and valleys throughout our lives. However, the limits I chose to experience are a bit further outside the comfort zone than most. This can prove to be a double-edged sword. When deciding to go against the norms of society, you take countless risks. A risk to become isolated, a risk to fail, a risk of injury, everything becomes a risk. From my perspective, not taking that risk would erase the opportunities that only appear when you're out on that ledge alone. That's when you learn your true identity and who you really are as a human being. For many, myself included, this can be quite frightening.

I do not, nor have I ever, recommended people try to live as I do, but I know there are many people I have met along my journey who make my stories seem tame. It's really perspective, and how far you want to push yourself in this life. The truth is that you will only grow when you are outside your comfort zone. This book fully attests to that, as many of my stories, I am operating in the "gray zone" in a world of black and whites. To me, this is a balance. That same balance required to perform a wheelie on a smooth straightaway, the same balance that has you levitate effortlessly with perfect buoyancy 30 meters under the ocean's surface. It's all just balance.

Even though some of these stories seem reckless, I take risk management quite seriously. I spend countless hours preparing, assessing, and researching every possible known situation, and even a few potential unknowns. Still, being fully exposed in the real world during these adventures, I understand the hazards and know that at any given moment it can all be taken away, but isn't that the point of living?

The key takeaway I want readers to feel after reading this book is that greatness is always on the other side of fear (possibly death). What you do in the face of that fear is what separates a mediocre life from a great life. We each have a voice inside of us that guides us towards our authentic self. Once we decide to take those steps - perhaps at first slowly and cautiously - towards our authentic self, the rest naturally falls into place. Eventually, the unknowns become familiar and even routine in some cases. Living in a bubble on your couch watching television is no way to experience our short time on this Earth. It's important to understand that there is never failure in trying something new. Even if you feel you failed miserably, you took the time, made the effort, and attempted an endeavor that many choose not to. It is that effort that needs to be rewarded more than the outcome of success or failure.

In short, enjoy these stories, don't take life too seriously, and most importantly, have fun.

The Motorcycle Stories

My First Motorcycle Arrest

Instead of the usual rah-rah stories on riding motorcycles, I felt the right way to fire this book off would be by highlighting some of my "shortcomings" with motorcycling. Many of us, when starting with this magnificent hobby, will experience a few blunders along the way and well... Some of us have had more significant blunders than others. Being who I am, it seems that when I do anything, it is usually to the extreme. Over my 30 years of motorcycling, it is pretty obvious that this activity would prove no different in me testing the boundaries, which can (does) result in crossing a line or two, but it wouldn't be a story if that weren't who I am.

I was a young U.S. Army Specialist serving in the 82nd Airborne Division. One of my best friends was about to go through a rough divorce at the same time that I felt the call to obtain my first motorcycle. He let me practice on his bike and use it for the test if I purchased it from him. Facing an imminent divorce allowed for an extremely generous discount (he needed divorce and beer money), and being flat broke, this was what led me to make the purchase. The bike was a bright yellow Honda Magna 750 that had more than enough power (probably too much) for a first motorcycle.

The deal was pretty much done. I passed my written test and was ready to take my driver's exam. I'm not sure if I was nervous or inexperienced (or both), but as soon as I started the test maneuvering around cones, I knew I was making a ton of mistakes. The Honda Magna was heavy and not the best choice for a new rider taking the motorcycle license test. Amazingly, though, I passed the exam. I later learned my friend had been chatting up the evaluator while I was testing to distract him.

Regarding a successful test output, my friend had as much skin in the game as I did. After passing the test, I paid him $3500 in cash that I obtained by somehow qualifying for a personal loan. I became the proud owner of a 1995 Honda Magna 750!

It didn't take long to realize I was invincible on the Magna, even though I had no riding skills. I was a 22-year-old unstoppable 82nd Airborne Paratrooper with a fast motorcycle. What could go wrong?

Pretty much everything could go wrong. Almost every evening, when leaving Ft. Bragg, there would be lights flashing in my rearview mirrors. It couldn't be for me, as I was too far ahead of them. This, of course, was because I was going over 100 miles per hour. Everything was distant in my rearview mirror at that speed. From what others had told me, the MPs were not allowed to leave post and had to call any pursuits into the local Fayetteville police. By the time that happened, and an officer would be dispatched, I was long gone and most likely home on my couch watching TV and having a beer.

This cat-and-mouse game went on for months. Not daily, but usually one or two times every week. I didn't care as it was nothing but entertainment for me. These near run-ins with the law helped my ego, but did not improve my riding skills. It was only a matter of time before the birds came home to roost.

Sitting at a light on Ft. Bragg, I decided to teach myself how to split lanes—not noticing an MP (a Military Police officer) nearby, and noticing even less the car driver next to signaling the MP. Instantly, the lights flipped on, and I heard the "whoop whoop" of a siren. This happened at the moment the light turned green. All traffic stopped to allow the MP to move forward, but he couldn't as everyone had frozen (except for me, of course). Clicking down into first gear and blasting off like a Shillelagh missile, I was out of there. Knowing the MP would be able to catch up quickly (I was in the heart of Ft Bragg), there was no running to the safety of the post border. After a quick couple of turns, I realized it was probably best to pull over.

It was no surprise that the MP was not too happy. As he was listing my charges, I asked him if I could go inside my battalion headquarters to let my team know I would be late returning from lunch. The MP agreed, and I entered the headquarters building and proudly announced, "Hey, Sarge, I am gonna need a little longer lunch today."

My sergeant asked why, and the MP promptly and quite loudly said, "His ass is coming with me to the station!" As I rode to the MP processing station and received my charges, it hit me: It was my wedding anniversary. Since my CQ (Charge of Quarters) shift was 24 hours, I hadn't called my wife. While the arresting officer was rambling to everyone in the station about my reckless driving, I thought this would be a good time to call her. I asked and was granted permission to make a phone call. I called my wife and wished her a happy anniversary. She was quite pleased that I somehow found the time to call during my busy day. The call was going great until my wife asked where I was.

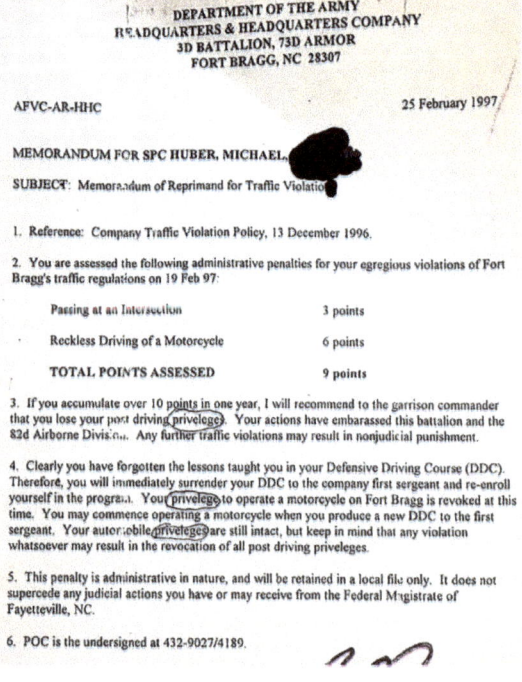

"Ummm, jail," I said. "I am in jail."

My wife was instantly very mad at me. Before that, she had been happy. I'll never understand women.

Once released from jail, I was not punished, other than receiving a written letter stating that I had embarrassed the battalion and the 82nd Airborne Division:

The letter was quite stern. I could not ride a motorcycle on Ft Bragg until I completed a motorcycle training class. The safety class was sorely needed, as my riding skills were horrendous (to say the least). The one hope I had was that upon completing the training class, my new riding skills would be used for good and not evil. Sadly, there would be a Part 2, a Part 3, and even possibly a Part 4 to my maturing as a motorcyclist. For the time being, however, I was allowed back on post, and I didn't receive any military judicial punishment; that was something to be thankful for.

Romanian Roaming 1: The Transfagarasan Highway

Like many of you, I seek out the most beautiful and exciting roads to experience on two wheels. Whenever possible, I try to achieve this on a Global level and not limit this quest to just my state or even my country. This isn't always the easiest objective to achieve. Many roads that are the pinnacle of any rider's dreams are usually quite far off the beaten path. This can seem like a deterrent to many, but my mindset is that using the distance to reach these places only adds more depth to the adventure. This will add both in miles, but new friends, and stories with each road you venture down.

If you perform a Google search on "best motorcycle roads on Earth" or any similar phrase, what will appear before you in the top images will be a photo of the Transfagarasan Highway. This mind-blowing highway is nestled deep in the Transylvania Mountains of Romania and was a four-day ride from Krakow, Poland. This is where I rented a Honda CBX600 motorcycle.

The day began with waking up in a yurt at an amazing moto camp in Sibiu, Romania. This moto camp is hosted by Doru Dobrota, has become part of Eastern European motorcycle folklore. Doru has been running this camp out of his family's old mountain cabin for years, and over that time has meticulously grown the camp to a perfect launching point to the many beautifully challenging roads of Romania. Upon finishing breakfast, it was confirmed that the weather would be cooperative. I just required some routine maintenance checks on the bike and a quick chat with some other riders staying at the camp, and I was ready to set out for one of the greatest days possible on a motorcycle.

It was a two-hour ride through some remote Romanian villages that required alertness throughout them due to deer, cattle, horses, and the usual obstacles to dodge around as I traveled from Sibiu to the base of the mountain pass, where the roads were already starting to become fun. Once the switchbacks began in the lower parts of the pine forests, I quickly twisted the throttle. I leaned into the perfectly paved corners as I began to ascend the highway to where you eventually are at the bottom of what would be like, in skiing terms, a giant bowl. Looking up, I am instantly in awe of what looks like a gigantic matchbox car racetrack recklessly thrown together by a 6-year-old.

After regaining my emotions from the ride that lies before my eyes, I jump on the Honda and hit the throttle hard. The road has nonstop switchbacks, but since it's so open, it allows you the ability to constantly overtake any vehicle in front of you easily. This enables me to really lean deep into each corner, pushing the red line of my little Honda, as well as challenging my own riding abilities. As I continue to traverse the switchbacks for what seems like forever, and just as it is about time for a break, I summit the pass, and stop for a quick breather at a waterfall to absorb the never-ending views of mountains and the pavement that was just completed. I can only imagine what remains in store for me as this perfect day is about to continue.

The southern side is where the descent begins. It is less dramatic, but it possesses spectacular views for miles until you snake below the tree line. Once there, you become absorbed back into the tight turns within the pine forest. The ride was going seamless when out of the corner of my left eye I spotted something crawling onto the road. At this point, I noticed the road had some sand on it, so my speed was only around 25MPH. My first thought was a small deer, but when I was finally able to decipher what it was, I had to stop and shake my head. It was a grizzly bear eating a bagel. Now that is something you don't see every day, and it was well worth stopping for a photo of. As I am taking the picture, I glance in front of me and see three more grizzlies. What was so concerning at this point was that they consisted of a mother bear and two cubs, which were fully blocking the road. So, I have one bear next to me eating a bagel and 3 in front of me. I hang my head down and reply to myself with my usual response to when I am in a bad situation, "So this is how it ends…" I decided to sit extremely still on the bike for a few minutes until the bears dispersed in front of me, retreating into the thick pine forest.

As the sunlight (and local wildlife retreated into the dense forests, I was still admiring the beauty of the road and what Romania had shined upon me this day. After a fresh fish dinner and the semi comfort of a hostel bed, I was able to fully absorb and appreciate the experience of riding one of the greatest roads on Earth, the Transfagarasan Highway.

Romanian Roaming 2: The Transalpina Highway

I awoke again in Moto Camp, located in Sibiu, just before sunrise. Moto Camp is probably the best base camp I have ever had. There wasn't much more one could ask for when staying near the Transylvanian Mountain passes are home to several of the World's most sought-after motorcycle roads.

While researching the weather, drinking a strong cup of Romanian coffee, it looked like this day would be promising, and it seemed that the weather forecast would provide me with a green light for riding. The buzz from riding the Transfagarasan Highway the day prior was still with me, and I was excited to see how the Transalpina Highway would rate in comparison.

The Transalpina Highway was about two hours away from Moto Camp. Before leaving, I searched out the least traveled roads to ride. These roads provided endless entertainment while passing through tiny villages that were untouched by time. Horse-drawn carts rolled along next to me, and the occasional sheep herd crossings reminded me I was indeed motorcycling in Romania. These sites were common to

Romanians, but to me, it was like stepping back in time to the early 1900s. Between the ever-changing scenery and the motorcycle engine humming, it was the perfect mesh of culture and time that merged nicely together into the present moment.

The small towns finally gave way to remote pine forests that were speckled with Beech trees and their shedding leaves. As the Honda sped by, the now rustled leaves began to create mini sparkling whirlwinds in the morning sunlight while I was accelerating into the sweeping corners of this magical road. After 30 minutes, I pulled into a rest stop along a dam with food and souvenir kiosks to grab a snack and drink. While sitting there, I noticed about 40 Porsches pulled up and took up the entire length of the dam. "Porsche Club of Romania" was stickered on the sides of their cars. Not wanting to be stuck behind any of the traffic, I began to eat with a purpose and prepared to tackle the second portion of this road.

Once leaving the dam, the sweeping corners continued, but with a steeper gradient, that were angled such that you really had to lean into them and keep your speed up while doing some geometry on the fly to avoid falling over. I continued to gain elevation while performing calculations on the angled corners when suddenly a bolt blew by me on the left, then another, and another. It was the Romanian Porsche Club; it seems they wrapped up their snacks at about the same time I had. As they roared past me, even on blind corners like a group of orcas going in for the kill, I thought, "Hey, I still have my Boston blood in me, I can be an apex predator as well", and I began to ride with them in formation as we roared past numerous other cars that were on their Sunday drive.

Having been so engrossed with the Porsches, the road beneath me, and my mind working geometry problems for the corners, I hadn't noticed how quickly the terrain had changed, yet again—this time, from pine forests to open alpine meadows with volcanic lakes beneath me. I continued to ride along these alpine meadows as a heavy fog began to move in. The road now was just over 5,200 ft. in elevation, but it felt like I was on top of the World. As I adjusted to the new terrain, the fog banks began to encircle me, and eventually, it got to a point where the visibility was down to almost zero. Then, just as quickly as the fog appeared, it retreated. When this happened, it was like the lifting of a veil to show a snapshot of the road ahead. It was important to remember that snapshot for future reference, for when the veil would once again lower over me.

Once hitting Ranca, which was the recommended turnaround point for the day, the fog began to roll in so heavily that even the Porsche club had turned around to retreat to lower elevations. Grabbing another break and sitting along a wall, I was fully able to absorb the view while still hearing in the distance the Porsche engines roaring as they continued their predatory ways back down the pass, while occasionally peeking in and out of the fogbanks. With the fog not seeming to be in a hurry to leave, it was a good time to return to the camp in Sibiu and mark off another incredible day of riding one of the best motorcycle roads in the Romanian mountains, the Transalpina Highway.

Vietnam: Charlie Don't Wheelie

In 2019, just before COVID slammed the world by stopping most travel while adding uncertainty, panic, and fear, I completed a 1,500+ mile motorcycle journey through the heart of Central Vietnam.

Asia. The largest continent in the World. Where the cultures are as vast as the geography, it had been some time since I was on this continent, and the first time was purely by a decision that there would be better stories out of Asia than where I was supposed to be stationed, which was Texas.

It was 1993, and I was graduating from AIT (Advanced Individual Training) as a U.S. Army Communications Specialist at Ft. Gordon in Augusta, Georgia. It was August, and the heat and humidity were brutal.

We were called into formation on this day, and we were given our orders for our first assignment as soldiers. As the Drill Sergeant called us up one by one, the anxiety in the air was intense. Would we go to Germany, remain in the United States, or maybe go to Korea? Most of us received stateside duties. As I eagerly opened my envelope, I learned my assignment was to report to Ft Hood, Texas. I was not happy at all, as my "Dream Sheet" consisted of Jamaica, Aruba, and Portugal (I figured, why not try for a cool duty station even though I knew it was extremely unlikely).

The formation dispersed after about 15 minutes, and I noticed one of my peers on the burnt lawn looking distraught. He was set to be married and his fiancée was pregnant, and he now had orders to Korea for a year. It took me all of 2 seconds to look at him and say, "Hey, wanna trade?" After a short chat with the Drill Instructor, we made it happen. I often wonder how his days in Texas went, but I find it hard to believe it could have been more of an adventure than what was to be my first duty station as a soldier in the United States Army.

I got what I was looking for: A lot of stories and a hell of an adventure in Korea with the 2nd Infantry Division. I was posted in Korea's demilitarized zone for a year. This story came to mind in December of 2019 as I groggily stepped off an airplane into the hot humidity of Da Nang, Vietnam, to spend 3 weeks motorcycling around the country along the Ho Chi Minh Trail. It had been a long 26-hour trip from Los Angeles to what I was about to realize was a beautiful and unique country. The Vietnamese culture, although extremely stunning, was much different from how Westerners live. To see it from a motorcycle was an adventure that few people experience.

As soon as I landed in Da Nang and got my bearings (as best I could with the jet lag, language barrier), the first step was to pick up the motorcycle from Tigit, the motorcycle rental company. I had reserved a Honda Winner 150cc motorcycle a month prior. I had some reservations about the smaller displacement, but the benefit of these little workhorse bikes was that the parts were so plentiful in the country, and they were so easy to work on that if/when I did break down, it wouldn't stall the trip for more than a day or two. This was an advantage compared to other models that you'd have to order parts and wait 3 or 4 days for even little maintenance issues. In hindsight, this was a wise decision, as I really beat the hell out of the bike.

The rental process with Tigit was painless, and with the owner giving me his WhatsApp contact number in case of breakdowns or other issues, I instantly felt comfortable in this new foreign land. Knowing the road conditions would be challenging, I also opted to bring all my protective gear from home. Once I was all geared up, it was time to ride!

The first destination would be a local beach in Da Nang. The wind and sun were just what was needed to flush out the jet lag and wooziness in my body.

In being true to myself, I had to decorate the bike. I had just recovered from a hip replacement in which I had a walker for a few weeks and decked it out with a bicycle bell, pink horn, pink streamers, and a pink basket. The nurses loved it, and old ladies in their walkers would give me dirty looks as I went about my errands on it (they were clearly jealous). I had reasons for these decorations, more than just an opportunity to be obnoxious. The bell was to signal I wanted pain meds, and the horn was for a cold beer. The streamers….well, they just seemed to tie the entire walker together. I brought them all to Vietnam to ensure my moto was properly suited to me. It provided endless entertainment for me and proved to be rather annoying to everyone else. Whenever I parked the moto, it just took a moment before children, police, or pretty much any local would be ringing the bell or honking the horn. On more than one occasion, my hosts had me park the bike inside their houses just so they could get a reprieve from the sounds of these add-ons. That benefitted me from a physical security standpoint.

At the start of this adventure, I felt a strange uneasiness. This came from notions placed in my head by others telling me about their experience during the Vietnam War. Feelings of guilt were constantly weighing on my mind as I met the locals and they asked where I was from. I was always extra respectful and humble when I said I was from the United States. Having travelled much of the world, this is always how I present myself, but in Vietnam, I did so even more. After a day or two, I began to open up with several Vietnamese people about how I was feeling (I am a pretty open guy anyway, so I wanted to get this heavy feeling resolved). They all assured me that the people of Vietnam have long forgotten about the war and that there would be absolutely no animosity over that from anyone. It didn't take long for me to put those feelings in the rear-view mirror. I began to fully embrace the beautiful people and their culture, as I should have from the start. As I continued to ride through the country, this became even more apparent with every stop; the local men invited me to sit on the stairs with them and smoke tobacco in bamboo pipes. Sometimes it just takes a day or two to get comfortable with your surroundings. Vietnam was no different.

I love it when a plan comes together, or doesn't. This is an especially great feeling when the plan is not to have a plan, other than a direction to travel in. For me, this direction was north. The goal was to hit the Vietnam North Pole, a remote area at the northern tip of Vietnam that bordered China. I had seen and read a lot about the roads up there, and it seemed like one of the most epic adventures a motorcyclist could have. During this journey, I wanted a leisurely pace with no pressure to travel if I didn't feel like moving due to being tired or falling in love with a specific region. Why rush this wonderful experience without savoring each mile to its maximum? The only constraint was to make my flight in Hanoi in three weeks, and this was plenty of time to cover 1,500 miles of the infamous Ho Chi Minh Trail if I chose to.

I was ready to begin the adventure. With my route defined as "sorta north", it was time to fire off this trip. I did this by starting in the wrong direction (south), and the reason for that was that Hoi An was close to Da Nang. There was a full moon festival happening there. This was something not to be missed.

Arriving in the bustling town of Hoi An late in the day, I noticed that the roads had been closed in a perimeter around my Home Stay (Vietnamese version of Airbnb) due to the Full Moon Festival. The Home Stay was about a quarter mile away from the closest point I could get to. Leaving the bike outside this perimeter wasn't an option, nor was walking a quarter mile through the crowds with all my gear. Having lived in Boston for 16 years, my driving style on a normal day was already quite aggressive, so I thought I would use that to my advantage.

I clicked the bike into first gear and drove across the bridge to the Home Stay, on the sidewalk, and on the wrong side of the road while honking my favorite pink horn to alert those in my path that I was coming through. The smile on my face was one that I'll never forget.

This country was one of fewer rules and more of making it happen. I loved it! Arriving at the Home Stay in time to unpack, catch my breath, and have a well-earned cold Saigon beer before heading out to find some chow.

Once properly hydrated from the Saigon beers, I walked the crowded streets of Hoi An as the glowing red sun began to set. I gazed over the beautiful Hoi An River. The river was filled with thousands of lanterns on tiny paper boats with candles, paying respects to ancestors. This was a sight to behold. It was beautiful in every way. As the night wore on, my grumbling stomach reminded me it was time to experiment with the Vietnamese cuisine.

Street vendors lined the alleys. They all had interesting dishes ranging from octopus to frogs that looked like Mr. Olympias (due to their muscles under the vendors' lights) to the quail that were runner-up to the frogs in the bodybuilding contests. Fried octopus seemed like the best choice. I ordered and sat at tables the same size used in preschool, with bright colors and flimsy plastic chair legs. The food was DELICIOUS and just what I needed after a successful first day of riding in this wonderful country.

Hoi An was an easy city to love, so it wasn't a hard decision to extend my stay. The next day entailed a full day of riding to a UNESCO World

Heritage Site called My Son Temple. This is a collection of Hindu temples hidden in the mountains 25 miles west of Hoi An. The site was incredible, with temples half overrun by the jungle, yet still in pristine condition, even though some of them are 600 years old. This location is deep in the jungle, and as soon as I dismounted from the bike, I could feel the humidity. I spent much of the day exploring the ruins, with the overwhelming jungle darkness surrounding me. The ruins were a mystical place that I was fortunate to have stumbled upon.

On the return ride, it was time to make food choices again. Choosing to stop at the first crowded place made sense. I soon discovered an establishment that looked acceptable. Instantly, all eyes were upon me as I sat down in a three-walled, white-paint-chipped open room. One thing I found in Vietnam was that when you order food, you don't always get what you asked for. Often, you get what they have, even though they will nod their head to your request while saying "ya ya ya." In this restaurant, I kept it simple and ordered pho.

While waiting for the food, I slowly drank a Hanoi beer that was warm, but much needed. I tried to act normal as the locals pointed at me and chuckled. Finally, my food arrived, but instead of the requested pho, I received what appeared to be cold water buffalo meat wrapped in a type of Vietnamese lettuce, a dipping sauce of some sort, and a consommé. Eating with finesse isn't my strong suit, and that became blatantly obvious. I was having issues making a wrap without having the meat spill out of the lettuce.

As all the patrons continued to stare at me, an older lady came over to assist me properly in preparing this dish, since I was clearly incapable of doing so myself. She began wrapping it tightly with her hands that were blackened with dirt from working in the rice fields earlier, and she successfully rolled it tightly for me to eat. While she was performing this task, other patrons in the restaurant were walking around me to go on the other side of the wall from where I was sitting to use the "facilities." With the sound of urine hitting the other side of the wall, it was now time to finally eat my lunch. I bit into the wrap and noticed the meat was cold, and I instantly thought it was raw and I'd get sick, but I still had to eat it to save face in front of everyone as they watched me chew each bite and swallow it. The many onlookers gazed upon me as I finished about 60% of the meal while washing it down religiously with Hanoi beer, thinking the alcohol might save me from becoming ill. For the next 12 hours, I was in full-on hypochondriac mode. I had about six false alarms during this time when I would bolt to the bathroom, thinking I was about to have an accident. In hindsight, this is funny, but at the time, the threat of possibly having the runs while riding through Vietnam didn't seem too humorous to me.

Returning to the Home Stay in Hoi An provided me with a bit of relief from my hypochondria and a chance to unwind. It was now time to map the next day's ride, where I would correct the direction and return to moving north towards epic roads. With the gear fully organized and the bike prepped, I called it an early night so I would be fresh for the following day.

By Day 3, I was fully acclimated to the roads, food, and culture, and it was now time to start taking on more challenging rides. The next day entailed leaving Hoi An to continue north to Hue for a couple of days. Along the way, I detoured to experience riding across the Hai Van Pass. According to locals, this was one of the best motorcycle roads in the country, if not all of Asia.

As I entered the Pass, there was a police road stop, and I was waved over instantly. "Ahhh, I've got this", I thought, thinking I would play the dumb tourist and skate out of any ticket. Well…it half worked. As soon as I began performing my best "sad tourist, I don't speak Vietnamese" act, the officer pulled out his phone with Google Translator. "Shit," I thought, this isn't going to turn out too great. Within a couple of minutes, another officer was called over. "Dammit!" I now thought, this definitely isn't how it is supposed to go down. It turns out I meandered into a lane that wasn't designated for motos. The other reason was that the officers wanted to honk the pink horn attached to my moto and take some photos with me. That was pretty cool.

Once my introductions to the local authorities were wrapped up, I continued to the base of the Hai Van Pass. By this time, I felt very comfortable in my riding abilities in Vietnam. It was just like riding a local road in the US: Leaning, feeling, and embracing each moment while blasting (blasting for a 150cc bike, by the way) into the corners while traversing the mountain passes. As soon as I gained my confidence in riding in this country, I received a big wake-up call. This was in the form of trucks passing recklessly on blind corners. I labeled these trucks "Terminators" based on my experience driving Humvees near the DMZ in Korea.

After completing the Hoi An Pass, I hit a new alertness level. A rule of thumb became that around every corner, expect a Terminator to be coming at you head-on, and always have a second path of egress when (not if) they do. This stayed with me as the Honda continued winding north to the Hoh Chi Minh Trail.

These cautionary actions didn't mean I wasn't having fun. As I entered the city of Hue, I noticed the bike was riding quite rough, as if the shock was just gone. It turns out that my showing off for the locals in traffic by performing wheelies and endos had caused the shock to go a bit sooner than anticipated, and fluid was leaking out. It was time to find a repair shop, as this wasn't something that would be tolerable for another 900+ miles. Fortunately, Hue is a large city, and while working with the rental company, Tigit, they quickly referred me to a local mechanic named Mr. Kim. As I explained the situation to him (I left out the wheelie part), I could hear all the mechanics honking the pink horn on my bike in the back. One thing about Vietnam: They get things done, and fast. Within two hours, Mr. Kim had rebuilt the shock and "bike all fixed, Mr. Hooba, no more bouncy bouncy." Upon arrival to pick up the bike, I continued to hear the honking of my horn in the back of the shop prior to them rolling it out. The shock was repaired, and I could continue the ride with a few less wheelies along the way.

With another obstacle (self-induced) behind me, I continued to Khe Sanh. Khe Sanh looks as though it hasn't changed one bit since the war. Gray concrete buildings line the streets, the smell of smoke from trash burning hung in the air, there were very few shops, and there were even fewer people along the main street through the center of town. To add to this gloomy scenario, it was a dark, cloudy day, and I was freezing from the ride. The hotel I stayed in even had a chill that refused to leave and stayed with me throughout the evening. I began thinking about the soldiers who fought here 50 years ago and what their opinion of this town was, both then and now. The night was short, and after eating a warm bowl of pho, I returned to the hotel. I planned a longer ride the next day and wanted to be fully rested as I wandered deeper into this country of never-ending adventure.

I awoke in Khe Sanh and felt well rested, semi-warmed up, and ready to ride the 270 kilometers to Phong Nha. Phong Nha is home to an elaborate cave system I planned to spend a few days exploring it. As I rode, it wasn't long before the concrete jungle of Khe Sanh morphed into a natural jungle. The road I chose was a narrow two-way street for most of the ride with no traffic. In fact, on one stretch, I didn't see another car for 100 kilometers. There was nothing but jungle encroaching onto the roads and waterfalls splattering off the pavement, creating little rainbows. As I whizzed past the rainbows, their light patterns would change to create a magical view into the dense, lush jungle that surrounded me. Although I never saw anyone along this section, my rule of having an exit path never stopped in the rare event that a Terminator would come barreling at me around a blind corner. Other than being alert for that possible occurrence, this stretch of the Hoh Chi Minh Trail was a rider's dream. It was so isolated and quiet outside, the sound of the motorbike humming, but even that sound was overtaken by the hungry jungle. This dense jungle ate everything it could, including sounds.

The mountain roads provided beautiful switchbacks. I saw patchy rain clouds below me, eerily floating by before the jungle consumed them. This part of the Trail is so remote that I filled up water bottles with gas to ensure the bike wouldn't go thirsty since there were no gas stations. Continuing up and down through mountain passes until the sunlight faded, I finally dropped into a beautiful green valley. Water buffalo wandered into my path as the roads straightened and the jungles were replaced with open rice fields and farmers.

After a short bit, I saw beautiful mountains so steep and high they looked like giant green anthills surrounding me. As I stopped to check and confirm my directions to the Home Stay, I heard Buddhist chanting echoing in the mountains. The chanting reverberated off the mountains, and it was impossible to tell where it came from. It fully engulfed me to the point it was vibrating through my motorcycle and even through my body. It was incredible.

The beauty of Phong Nha was beyond description, so there was really no option but to extend my stay there by a day to have an opportunity to tour the Buddhist temple during their Moon ceremony. I explored and hiked many caves, including Paradise Cave, one of the largest in the world. The extra day provided a much-needed break from riding. Even 150 miles made for quite a day when you factor in researching the best routes, watching for Terminators, and taking in the culture and sights.

After three days in this magical location, it was time to load the moto up and roar off (as much as the little 150cc motorcycle could roar) in a northerly direction. With no defined stopping point on this day, it was exciting to see where the day would take me. This is never a bad way to travel and rarely fails to provide excitement. This case was no different, as I stumbled onto a beautiful eco lodge where I toured island tea fields by boat. At this lodge, German riders were going in the opposite direction. This started a great conversation on where to stay for myself going north, and for them going south. They showed a video of a rickety old bridge on where you could see the bamboo flipping up in all directions from the weight of the motorcycle. This bridge would be added to my route north. It also worked as it took me through a more isolated area, including Pu Luong National Forest. This forest had beautiful jungle mountain switchbacks. As a much smaller road, it would have fewer Terminators.

I arrived at the wobbly bridge late in the day and zipped across it several times. I laughed as I heard the boards clacking one by one when I crossed. It sounds silly, but this may have been my favorite part of the entire adventure to this point. The German riders gave me not only great advice on the bridge, but they also recommended a Home Stay next to the nature preserve. It had great food and all you can drink rice wine included. The beers were a bit bland, but the rice wine was just the change I needed to unwind, loosen up to chat (maybe too much) with the other guests, and enjoy the evening in a hammock after a fabulous Vietnamese dinner. This wonderful hidden gem of the world led me to extend my stay longer to explore the national forest and its lush waterfalls with my new friends.

Exposure is one of the greatest thrills when traveling by motorcycle. You feel every drop of rain and every cold or warm front you move through, experiencing each second by second. There is no better way to experience the present, except for maybe exiting an aircraft in flight. Being a motorcyclist and embracing that exposure allows for the most beautiful moments. During these moments, I sometimes close my eyes for an instant to ensure my mind has a vivid snapshot that can be stored deep within and recalled for the rest of my life. With this beauty, at times there comes a price, and at times that price can be death.

I was wrapping up the journey, having decided not to ride to the Vietnamese North Pole due to time constraints caused by meandering travels. Instead, I chose local mountain roads I found while planning this trip. This made for relaxed riding and an easy return to the Home Stay in Mai Chau. The roads were incredible, some just dirt, half covered by dirt avalanches that barely allowed scooting the little 150cc motorcycle through. Every so often, I would enter a village where pigs and water buffalo blocked the roads as children came out to honk the horn prominently taped to my handlebars.

After returning to the main road, just a few mountain passes away from Mai Chau, I decided to break for lunch. Older locals were drinking what looked like a Vietnamese vodka. Being ever curious about local drinks, I attempted to order a bottle (or two) to go. This took more than a few minutes. Vietnam has so many dialects that many revert to English as the communication platform, but not here. It took about five minutes and included several charades imitating the drunken locals I had just seen to obtain the right beverage. No question about it: My performance would be the talk of that local watering hole for some time.

I loaded the vodka bottles carefully into the plastic side panniers and fired up the moto. The narrow two-lane highway was stunning. There were beautiful mountain views and sheer cliffs to my right, where I could overlook the vistas and still see lingering fog far below me in a mystical valley. Traffic was light that day, but I was alert for Terminators barreling around blind corners and, as always, remained cautious.

Suddenly, a female with a pink Hello Kitty plastic helmet zipped by me on her scooter. I waved to her as we do to all riders and glanced again to look at the mountain views. I took a deep breath as I knew this would be one of those snapshot moments I wanted to remember forever. I didn't realize how right I was. In the very next moment, a Terminator was barreling directly at me in my lane, and I had no escape with the cliff on my right. Before I could react to anything, I heard plastic crunching and witnessed a body fly into the air just in front of me. The entire world stopped for a moment as the crescendo of a full orchestra built and screamed in my head. Then it suddenly stopped, and the only sound was the quiet sound of a gentle wind.

I parked the bike and ran over. The female rider was still breathing, but there was nothing that could be done. With traffic stopped, I knew that on these mountain roads, this scene would just get worse. I attempted to tell the driver to call 911, knowing that most of these countries don't have emergency services, but also knowing he wouldn't need to read my charades to know what action to take. I flipped my moto around and drove up a quarter mile and decided I would pull road guard detail to prevent other vehicles from piling into the already chaotic scene.

Road guard duty was not an easy task on that foggy mountain highway in Vietnam. I remembered I had downloaded Google Translate after being pulled over and quickly looked up "Stop bad accident ahead," but even with using Google Translate, the trucks continued to ignore me to the point that they were jeopardizing everyone currently at the accident scene. They continued to speed toward the horrific situation ahead. Some vehicles were even going off the road to the left to avoid the accident or the cliffs after ignoring my warnings.

Out of frustration and with no other option, I physically walked into the middle of the road using myself as a barrier to force each vehicle to stop (I hoped). This action ultimately worked, and the threat of new vehicles arriving at the accident site stopped.

Sometime between 45 minutes and a lifetime later, authorities arrived on the scene, but only in the form of a traffic officer on the back of a civilian moped. At this juncture, it was time for me to depart. There was nothing else I could do; the female rider had died, and it was time for me to leave. I slowly continued my ride down the pass and into the lowering mountain switchbacks and the cool fog of Mai Chau Valley. After 45 minutes of riding, an ambulance passed me heading to the accident. I knew there was no rush for the ambulance at this point.

With Mai Chau being in the rear view mirror, I just had one challenge left to overcome as a rider in Vietnam: The chaotic traffic in the massive capital city of Hanoi. This was something I was mentally prepared for and had watched videos to somewhat provide me with an idea of what to expect, but it would take more than me honking my little pink horn to navigate through this massive Asian city. As I rolled down the CT08 Highway into Hanoi, the road didn't seem too hectic, although I bounced off a car once or twice due to the limited real estate on the road.

Exiting the highway and entering surface streets, the traffic increased exponentially. The road was about four American lanes wide, but it easily fit 8 to 12 vehicles on average. The vehicles ranged from Terminators to cars to little motos like mine, and everyone was cutting in and out constantly.

Another valuable driving lesson I learned was not to drive defensively, but instead to drive with purpose and intent. In doing so, you will fit into the chaos and become part of the herd. Any second-guessing yourself, braking, or quick acceleration will cause a ripple effect. That action will initiate others to stutter step and will most likely result in an accident; this was something I would rather avoid. Having a mount for my phone was another tip that proved invaluable. I could set my directions into it and place the phone in airplane mode to preserve the battery. Google Maps would remain on and guide me through these crowded streets filled with threats and obstacles.

Even with the GPS reliably guiding me through the madness, I was rerouted several times due to the amount of traffic and losing focus due to the many distractions that came in every form from every direction. Negotiating the rotaries was like entering a swarm of bees and trying to fit into my own little pocket without disrupting thousands of others that were searching for the same sanctuary in the lunacy. Upon arriving safely at the rental moto return point, I dismounted from my reliable steed. The Honda Winner had been my life preserver over the past three weeks and 1,000+ miles through the concrete and plant jungles of this magnificent country.

This journey through Vietnam, as with most journeys, was challenging mentally, physically, and especially emotionally. Vietnam reassured my feelings that the division between cultures and former enemies can be cured. Time provides a buffer that often can mute anger and hatred. One given about traveling is that it can feel as though you time-travel. Helping a North Vietnamese would have been considered treason 70 years ago, but now helping someone was the only right thing to do. Hours after witnessing the accident in Mai Chau and the actions of others that day gave me hope that the political division in our country will be repaired. We are one people, and our minor differences are indeed that: Minor. We sometimes tend to focus on the differences when we should be focused on the similarities.

Take the Iwo Jima "replica" photo above. I was riding by, and a lady waved me down. They were planting a tree and were stuck, so I ran over without even taking off my helmet as it started to fall. We fixed it. A tree now grows in Vietnam, and I helped.

Zooming Through New Zealand

Having both traveling and motorcycling as my two greatest passions in life, whenever I have an opportunity to combine them, it is always quite magical. Add on top of that camping, and it's a trifecta for pure bliss. Having found myself in New Zealand and previously hearing tales of the incredibly technical roads and terrain here was something that I didn't want to miss, yet I almost did.

One of my strengths as a traveler, which seems counterintuitive, is my lack of planning. I rarely plan more than a week in advance, and sometimes less than that. In the past, this has been a double-edged sword. The agility of minimal planning allows me to instantly adjust with few consequences when opportunities arise, but it also has caused me to miss highlights that require more planning. Still, this is the way I have traveled, and for the most part it works. To be fully transparent, the lack of planning could be due to laziness. But to be perfectly honest, if it hadn't been at least semi-successful, I would absolutely put in the work to lay out a more detailed plan.

This lack of planning almost became a major regret here in New Zealand. By the time I arrived on the South Island to reserve a motorcycle, they were booked months in advance. I was pretty distraught, but I understood the reasoning since it was peak tourism season (and I hadn't planned). It didn't look like riding a motorcycle in New Zealand was in the cards for me.

There was a bright spot as an old friend of mine, Neal from the United States, happened to be on an Air Force duty assignment here. We hadn't hung out in almost 20 years, so seeing him would be a great way to wash away the disappointment. Neal was in Christchurch and attached to an Air Force unit whose mission was to provide support for Antarctica. I thought this was really cool, as they were part of the maintenance team for C-130s that delivered supplies to the frozen continent. I love C-130s as I used to jump out of them when I served with the 82nd Airborne Division. The only difference (from my limited perspective) is that the props had eight blades on the propeller instead of four, and these planes had skis attached to the wheels for ice landings. Of course, I thought all this was badass.

Leading up to our visit, Neal kept mentioning this Brazilian BBQ place that is an all you can eat meat on a stick fest. When we arrived, along with three of his soldiers, the owner came out to greet my friend like he was the mayor of Christchurch. Instantly, I knew Neal frequents this place quite often.

After we ordered Brazil's National Drink, the Caipirinha, we waited for the feast to begin. During this time, I began chatting up the owner. He was originally from Arizona and had motorcycled quite a bit throughout the United States. It didn't take long for the conversation to turn to motorcycling in New Zealand and how I couldn't find a bike.

Within 5 minutes, he had texted the owner of a local family-owned rental company, South Pacific Motorcycles. They had a BMW GS750 available for the exact days I wanted. This was great to hear. I may be able to rebound from my lack of planning after all! If this wasn't destiny, I don't know what is.

I had 5 days to kill in Christchurch until I picked up the BMW. That wasn't a problem, as it's a fairly large city with some quirky architecture, botanical gardens, museums, and beaches to occupy my time until it was time to pick the bike up. The downtime also allowed me to research different routes. This wasn't done by online forums or social media groups but by just looking at maps and putting a route together (as I would do in the United States). Again, this could be laziness, but it's what works for me. Things were looking bright, and the weather was great the day Kim, from South Pacific Motorcycles, picked me up in front of my hostel. It was time to get this adventure underway.

Kim from South Pacific Motorcycles had just picked me up at my hostel in downtown Christchurch, New Zealand, and we were off to meet my new steed for the week. It was a BMW GS750 named "Massie." Even with my lack of planning, somehow the Universe decided I needed to get back on a motorcycle, and I was fortunate enough to snag the last one available for the dates I was in town. The stars couldn't have aligned any better.

Kim and I exchanged ideas on routes and agreed that the one I had lazily researched would be great, but it might result in some long riding days. I would have to forego some hikes and tourist attractions that were on my list. It was a loop that would take me over three unique mountain passes, and allow me to see two glaciers and cruise along ocean roads. It would be a full riding trip with not much time for hikes and other tourist stops. This was fine with me as I was itching to ride again. Also, I had enough time remaining in the country that if anything appealed to me, I could always return via bus or rental car.

The weather was a perfect 70 degrees F, and I was ready to hit the switchbacks as I raced towards Arthur's Pass National Park. The roads were pretty solid going through this area. It was just exhilarating to be riding again (and in another country at that). In all my excitement and being so caught up in the moment that I forgot to top off on fuel before heading into the mountains. Fuel is something I am usually quite responsible with. A half tank is an empty tank in my mind, especially in a foreign land.

Upon hitting the first town after completing Arthur's Pass, Massie's fuel level read a mere 18km remaining (a rookie mistake by me). Once the bike was topped off, I sat under the gas station's awning to figure out where I would be staying that evening. The rental company recommended staying in Holiday Parks. These were similar to the KOAs that we have in the United States.

I cannot stand KOAs unless I was in a pinch that would not be my plan for the evening. Camping in New Zealand is different from the United States in that many areas are called "freedom camping," but to stay there, you have to have a self-contained vehicle sticker. To obtain the sticker, the vehicle must undergo a rigorous inspection process to ensure that the vehicle has a toilet in it. So, Freedom Camping was obviously out of the question.

Hunting down campsites wasn't anything new for me. It didn't take me long to remember that on the North Island, I had camped in DOC (Department of Conservation) campsites. These campsites could be quite primitive, but they have toilets, this meant I didn't require a sticker. I found them in really beautiful areas, and at a cost of just $15 NZD ($10 USD), they met all my requirements for a peaceful night of camping.

The campsite was spectacular. It was next to a beautiful lake with plenty of weka birds that would walk right up to you and hang out for a bit. It had been a short day, but it was the perfect length to get used to the bike, chat with a few other riders, and get back into camping off a motorcycle. I was back in my natural environment and decided to call it an early night. I knew the next day I would have to put some serious mileage behind me if I was to complete this loop.

There are certainly worse places to wake up. I opened my eyes facing a beautiful mountain lake with loud wekas clumsily hunting for food in the brush next to my tent. Without my cooking gear, it took me just about 20 minutes to pack up and load Massie, the BMW GS750, for what would be a full day of riding. As I was packing up, I was already craving a coffee and a meat pie for breakfast. While stuffing my gear in the panniers, I noticed how wet everything was from the dew with camping so close to the lake. The sun was out, though, so I thought after an hour or so of riding, I would dry it out as I ate breakfast.

Riding to breakfast took a bit longer than expected, and the one hour turned to three. Not that big of a deal, as the sun was fully out now and would allow for my gear to dry while I researched my route and stops for the day. As I pulled into a coffee shop in a small town along my route, the waitress stated that it would be a while for my food and coffee. This was my queue to unpack my wet gear and lay it out to dry while I was researching maps and things to do for the day.

During my wait, several people introduced themselves, and we had some fun conversations about my gear and riding. It was a great environment, or so I thought. After about 20 minutes, my coffee and food arrived, and I was told that maybe I should take it to go, and it was time to pack up my gear. I guess they didn't like the look of my tent and equipment drying and sprawled out all over their front porch. I sort of understood, even though many of the clientele had been chatting me up. I apologized and, well, it took me about as long to pack up that gear as it did for them to bring my coffee (it happened to be fully dry by the time it was packed). I found it a bit rude, but I understood that having my gear everywhere could be viewed as a bit of a mess. It was time to get going, anyway, as I had a long day ahead.

During my minimal research and planning at the coffee shop, I discovered this one hike that I continually heard about from others. It was the Mount Cook Hooker Trail. The hike wasn't too long, and it had an incredible view at the end. This was only a couple of hours off my planned route. Adding that hike meant I would have to have a long day and miss a lot of stops that tourists hit, such as the Franz and Fox Glaciers and hikes along that area. I decided to prioritize the Hooker Trail and skip the glaciers and other coastal hikes. Having made this decision meant a 350-mile day. To me didn't seem like a lot, but the roads were tight and windy, I thoroughly enjoyed these roads, probably too much, as I used the long day as a reason to really wear the edges of the tires in.

After close to 10 hours of aggressive riding through what I felt was like a mini version of the Western United States and British Columbia, I arrived where I thought I would camp for the evening, just outside a city called Wanaka. However, the "campground" resembled something of a tent city I would expect to find under Interstate 5 in Seattle. That made it a hard pass for me. I did have a second option, but it was another 45 minutes north, and if it didn't work out, I would be in a tight position as the day was beginning to wear on me. I decided to shoot for it and hope for the best. What I found was far more than I expected and maybe one of the coolest places I've ever moto camped.

It was well after 6:00 p.m., and I was starting to hit my wall for riding. My goal was to travel to this campground I stumbled upon on Google, it was about 5 miles down a dirt road, that had some decent reviews. The rental company mentioned no off-roading, as Massie had street tires. I zoomed in on the map and saw "Linda Road," so I technically was not off-roading. Check!

The road was a very tame forest service road with the occasional "Traffic Lamb," as quite frequently there were herds of sheep, and they would part like the Red Sea as they heard Massie's engine roar grow closer.

Once I neared the campsite, I noticed a couple of old, rundown stone buildings (from who knows how long ago) and a few van lifers dispersed around a large field. This was a really cool spot! Not only that, but you had views for miles of the sun beginning to set over the brown grassy mountains that surrounded the location. This was Linda's Camp. It was an old short-term gold mining operation from the 1860s, which switched hands a few times before finally being abandoned in the 1950s. This was an amazing place to camp, and it was far off the grid. I didn't even have cell service.

After setting up my tent, I struck up a conversation with an old gold miner. He was living in his van there and spent his days panning for gold off a nearby river with minimal luck. He got a good laugh from my story about getting the boot from the coffee shop earlier that day for drying my gear there. The rest of the evening was spent exploring the hotel ruins and a short hike up the mountain to watch the sunset.

Camping that evening was one of those moments where I really was able to relax, breathe, and be in the present. It was a long but rewarding day, and I thought having an early night was in order. It would be another long day tomorrow, including the Hooker Trail hike. This was the hike I was greatly looking forward to.

Waking up in yet another serene location with Massie sitting just outside the tent was another perfect kickoff to this new day. Since it was still pretty early, after packing, I thought pushing the bike out of the camping area was the proper thing to do to avoid waking any of the van lifers (or the gold miner).

Once well outside the perimeter, I went to start the bike. Nothing happened. Shit. The battery was somehow dead. I took the panniers off and attempted to manually jump-start it off a small incline. No good. It wasn't starting. Well, I thought, it was not so funny breaking that "stay on the road rule. I had no cell signal either. As I sat down, weighing my options (none of which were good), I heard a couple of pots banging together. The old gold miner was up. I walked over and asked if he had jumpers, and he did! Sure enough, the bike fired right up with his help. Okay, cool, I can still make the Hooker Trail even if I am an hour behind schedule. And, the rental company would never know I was off-road.

Once I was back on the main road and well on my way, the need for coffee hit me. I pulled into a rest area to see if there was a cell signal to guide me to a coffee shop. There was a cell signal, and there was a coffee shop not too far away. I pulled out and began racing the Linda Pass switchbacks when suddenly all I saw was a huge yellow Scania 18-wheeler coming head-on at me. Why was he in my lane? SHIT! I was on the wrong side of the road! In my morning fog and my distraction from the battery issue, I zoned out and drove on the right side of the road. Even with a giant yellow arrow on Massie's dashboard as a constant reminder, I somehow ignored the fact that they drive on the opposite side in New Zealand. I didn't have much time to react and managed to skirt along, not so much on a shoulder, but on a strip of grass as the truck blasted by me.

That was close. I really didn't need any coffee after that wakeup call, but what I did need was a moment to get my head back in the game (especially if I was to complete the Hooker Trail and find a campsite). Due to Massie's moody electrical system, tonight's campsite would need to be near a town with a strong cell signal. It was still early, and my confidence was high. I knew I would satisfy both objectives.

I was in the tiny town of Omarama, New Zealand, having coffee and trying to wake up enough to plan the day. I was under an hour and a half away from the Hooker Trail, that I had learned just a day or so ago was not too far off my original route. I normally avoid touristy places as much as possible. One of my many travel mantras is "If I run into another American, I have failed." That's because most Americans stay on the beaten path and rarely venture off, but venturing off always seems to be happier place for me.

As I finished my coffee and began to put my gear back on for the ride to the Hooker Trail, I fueled up since New Zealand was pretty devoid of towns for the next couple of hundred miles. These remote areas are perfect for riding. I was expecting Mount Cook would be similar to the other areas of New Zealand and was preparing to view a miniature copy of, say, Mt. Hood. The previous day (although incredible and diverse) was like a 70% replica of the western United States with a sprinkling of British Columbia thrown in. Yes, I am extremely spoiled in my perspectives on motorcycle roads. I understand this.

It didn't take long after leaving the coffee shop before low-level clouds consumed me and the road. I had just gone through a similar area and noticed that when I gained some elevation, it cleared up. I remained optimistic as I strained to see anything in front of me. The attempt to hike the Hooker Trail surely would be in vain if the weather continued to stay this way, as I have heard it often does up in the Southern Alps of New Zealand.

Fortunately, this wasn't the case. Once I hit Lake Pukaki, I had obtained enough elevation so that the clouds were below me. Lake Pukaki then came into full view, and it was stunning. The neon green water contrasted with the brown mountains surrounding the lake, and it became all I could see. The colors were so overwhelmingly bright I had to pull over several times, not only to take the views in but allow my eyes to adjust from the drab cloudbank that had engulfed me over the previous hour.

After another 30 minutes of riding along this other-worldly lake, I could see Mount Cook was getting close, and I was excited to finally hike the Hooker Trail. As I entered the parking lot around noon, I noticed how crowded it was. There was hardly any parking (at least for cars). I found a perfect spot for Massie right up front next to the trailhead and swapped out my riding outfit for hiking gear.

This was it: The Hooker Trail. It wasn't too long, only around 6 miles round trip. Once I began hiking, I understood why I had kept hearing about it in my travels and when reading random blogs and posts. It was super-crowded. The hike was beautiful. Around each corner was a new view of either glacial lakes or views of Mount Cook towering above. The trail ended at a glacial lake with a beach that was perfect for a quick swim. It was mid-afternoon, and it was warming up quite nicely.

Massie was parked right where I had left her and ready to blast out our final few hours to the hostel on the edge of Lake Tekapo. The trip had taken me through what felt like a whirlwind of geographical features. There's no question that the roads, people, and environment in New Zealand are a dream for anyone (especially a motorcyclist). As I cracked open a cold Kea IPA on the lakeshore, a sense of satisfaction came over me. I could now add New Zealand to the growing list of countries I have motorcycled. The memories of this trip will help me pass the time while on the long flight to my next destination. Cheers, New Zealand!

India: Prelude to Adventure

I first went to India in May of 2005. I was about to graduate from Boston University after nine long years (the 9-year part will probably make for another interesting story) and knew it was time for a well-deserved break. At this point in my life traveling abroad was new to me, and I thought India would make for an excellent adventure with all its beauty and intensity. This trip would also allow me to forego physically going to a boring graduation ceremony (even though it was my own).

I had NO idea what I was doing, as it was one of my first trips abroad outside of the Army. Well, the best way to learn is by falling and skinning your knees, and boy, my knees got torn up this trip (I am sure my paratrooper mates will have some smart ass remarks on that line). It was to be a once-in-a-lifetime adventure (well, twice in a lifetime now).

The trip didn't start smoothly. As we landed in Trivandrum, the southernmost tip of the country, I was exhausted since I had been up for 30+ hours. It was late May, and the weather was hot and humid. All I wanted to do was sleep in a hotel with air conditioning. Eventually, I got my wish and found a hotel room. As a foreigner, I was required to list my friend who was staying with his family as a reference. The hotel was located in a tiny village that was very remote. My friend pulled me aside as I was checking into the hotel and said he would pick me up in the morning "Don't do anything stupid" were his parting words that day. Tall order indeed, but I was wiped and figured that behaving wouldn't be too difficult.

When I awoke after a solid nap, I was hungry and thought I would get some food. I left the hotel still woozy from the long journey, but found a street cart with food. As I began eating, next to the food cart, I noticed quite a traffic jam building up. It seemed I was causing the traffic jam with all the attention I was drawing. They had never seen a white American before. Cars were stopping to take pictures of me, and numerous people approached to have conversations. After about an hour of talking and singing American music with them, it was time for me to return to my room for some more rest.

The following morning, my friend showed up mad as hell. "I told you not to do anything stupid." I was perplexed as to what he was referring to. Well, turns out I drew so much attention that an Indian Government Agency (he stated it was the equivalent of the FBI) had called him asking who I was and what I was doing in this remote Indian village. It was more of a health and wellness check than anything,

After a week, I parted ways with my friend and began traveling through northern India on my own. This was when I got my first solid

hit of culture shock, and it hit me big-time. Being alone and traveling through the bustling streets of Delhi, Agra (to see the Taj Mahal), and the Himalayan mountain town of Leh would prove to be a wakeup call that was clearly overdue. There were no cell phones or Google Maps to navigate by during this trip. Add to that the intensity of Delhi traffic and just the overall controlled chaos that overwhelmed every sense and came from every direction possible (and some directions I didn't even know existed). It was sensory overload to the point that one day, I cancelled all my scheduled tours and stayed in my hotel with the blinds down. It was that level of intensity just outside my hotel room. The mix of culture shock and wandering through these places alone made for anxiety I had never felt before. By the time I was packing to leave, I felt as though this country had overwhelmed me so much that I was questioning my confidence in traveling.

In February 2025, my flight approached Delhi, India, and the thoughts in my head began racing back to 2005 when I experienced culture shock for the first time. Being nervous, I was optimistic as I had a couple of things in my favor that I didn't have 20 years prior. That being technology with our phones and apps, and my experience over the past 20 years traveling to quite a few countries. I took comfort in that as the plane landed and pulled up to the gate.

The last time I exited the Delhi Airport, I was instantly mobbed by a crowd of taxi drivers pulling at my luggage and quoting me absurd prices for a ride to the hotel. This time was much different, and although there were Ubers, I chose to hire a taxi from the government taxi stand. Other than a few obvious scams, I was not bothered by anyone at all. It was quite a refreshing change, and after a 45-minute ride, I was dropped off at my hotel, where I could relax and slowly take in Delhi in a way I was not allowed to 20 years ago.

With memories still lingering from my previous experience in this country, I knew that the best way to overcome them was to embrace the culture, not shy away from it. For my first day in India, I would take a local bus. This would not only force me to get over these haunting feelings from the past but also enable me to gain my confidence in the most effective way possible. The bus was crowded, but not too overwhelming. It was a 30-cent ride versus a $3 Uber.

With my renewed confidence in my ability to navigate through this beautiful but chaotic city the following day I chose to take the subway to

Iqbal Motors. Iqbal Motors is the company we would be renting our Royal Enfield Himalayas from. The train was a bit more crowded than the bus. To the point when I finally found the correct subway (on my third try, but hey, I was learning, so I went easy on myself), The train was packed, to the point where I really had to squeeze into the subway car. It was a tight fit, but not that bad, until the doors opened at the next stop. Not fully paying attention, the next thing I knew, I was thrown about 15 feet from the train and was well onto the platform before I realized I had to fight crowds to make it back onto the train prior to it leaving. Not wanting that to happen again, I fought my way to the center of the car and faced towards the doors that would open for my stop. Now it was my turn. As soon as the doors opened, I crouched down into a sort of rugby scrum stance and pushed with all my might to exit the car. Success! I was out and just a few blocks from Iqbal Motors.

I was excited to finally meet Iqbal at his shop and check out our new 2025 Royal Enfield Himalayans. The bikes were beautiful, and the communication over the previous two months with Iqbal on fine-tuning our needs for gear, schedules, and overall itinerary made an otherwise challenging rental easy. I knew we made the right decision as soon as I met him. I cannot say enough good things about Iqbal and his motorcycle rental company.

Upon saddling up on the Himalayan and taking the bike out for a short blast, I instantly understood why this was the chosen motorcycle for India. All my apprehensions and anxiety about this trip melted away as I zipped through traffic in Delhi. I was officially excited and ready to spend the next three weeks (or longer) on my new steed. My friends were set to arrive in two days, and I was ready to begin this motorcycle adventure through the crowded, yet mystical country of India.

My third day in India: I bought new motorcycle gear (helmet, jacket, gloves, all for $73 USD). I am not saying this gear was high-end Aria or anything, but it was something. In the event of a crash, I would hope it would be low speed, and I could count on my paratrooper skills to fall properly and not get too banged up. Things were coming together nicely, and my confidence and morale were much higher than I had expected.

With an extra evening to kill, it turned out one of my offshore developers who worked with me in 2014 lived in Delhi and had invited me over for dinner.

When I was in corporate America, I loved hanging out with my team whenever I wasn't out roaming around the world. Well, when I met this guy, he had just gotten off the plane in Seattle, and it was his first time in the United States. Knowing this, I directed another one of my team members to pick him up and bring him to Pike Place Market, where we could get a few beers and I could fully christen him to our great country.

Of course, my idea for the full American immersion was to bring him to a proper strip club that was next to Pike Place Market. Without getting into details, he probably had one of the best nights of his life. We kept in touch over the years, and whenever I would walk by the strip club, I would send him a photo of the sign, and that is how you maintain high morale on a project team (leadership at its finest).

I arrived at his apartment and met his lovely wife and sister-in-law. After catching up and chatting for an hour, they invited me to their parent's home for dinner. The conversation then turned to birthdays, and they asked when mine was. I pulled out my phone and looked at it intensely. They didn't know what I was doing, as I should have known my birthday (which I did). They were surprised to hear my next words: "My birthday is in 3 hours and 42 minutes."

I don't know a lot about the Indian culture, but within two minutes, I had a birthday cake in front of me, so I am guessing they always have a birthday cake in the freezer "just in case." Either way, it was very sweet and I felt more than welcomed into their country.

After a few pre-birthday whiskeys, it was time to return to my hotel and get a solid night's sleep. I needed to wash away any remaining jet lag I had as my friends were due to arrive the following day. As I peacefully fell asleep with thoughts of riding the new Royal Enfields, my phone rang. "Huber, I need a place to sleep!" Well, I guess I would be meeting at least one of my new friends sooner than expected as I buzzed the hotel door to let him in. It turned out his hotel had given his room away, so we would be roommates until we departed on the motorcycles in two days.

India: Rolling South

The next day was the day we would pick up the Royal Enfield Himalayas. I was excited to show my new riding partners the bikes, having taken them out a couple of days prior. We all met at Iqbal's motorcycle shop bright and early. As we unpacked our gear and transferred it from boxes and backpacks into the panniers and saddlebags, I noticed one thing: They had a LOT of gear. This wasn't a bad thing, as I was missing a lot of necessities such as tire repair kits, jump starters, and tool bags. As I looked over at my moto and the gear I had, I realized it was pretty limited, which at first glance had me concerned, but then, after thinking it through, I thought: How many tire repair kits do you really need?

After wrapping up the final paperwork with Iqbal, we suited up and were off. It would be a short day with just a little over four hours of riding. This was perfect, as it took an hour to navigate through Delhi, whiz through the suburbs, and eventually find our way into the country where we could relax while riding a bit. For me, the relaxation didn't really happen as I had no communication with the others, and my phone seemed to constantly go in and out of cell coverage. This meant that I had to keep an eye on at least one of the other two to avoid drifting off and getting lost. If nothing else, it was a motivator and solid excuse for my aggressive riding. At least that's what I told myself.

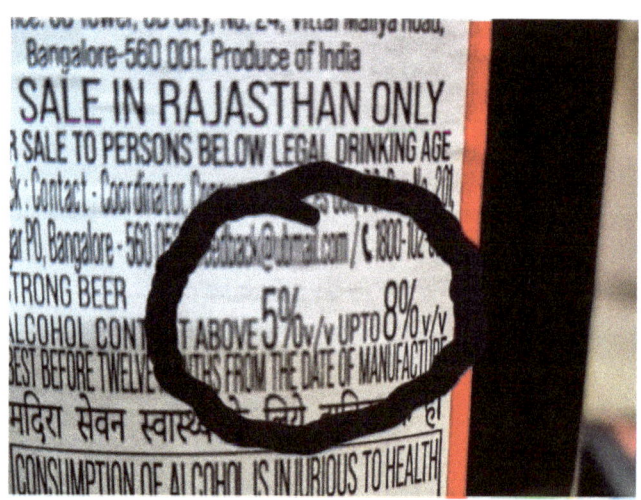

Around 15:00 we decided to call it a day, get a hotel, some food, and a couple of beers in a tiny town called Alawar. I say a couple of beers because the local beers (called Kingfisher) were a crapshoot with regard to how strong they were. They fluctuated between 5% and 8% ABV (alcohol by volume), so until you had one, you really didn't know which end of the spectrum you would end up on. This was a nightly roulette game where we would play "who got the 8% beer?" Over the next few weeks, we all had our time with the 8% beers at one point or another. This added yet another unknown into our travel equation (as if we needed any more unknowns), but it was fun nonetheless at the end of a long day of riding.

Another interesting nightly game was "Which switch controls the lights?" It seemed that every room had at least two panels with a minimum of six switches per panel. This made turning the lights out each evening about as doable as solving a Rubik's Cube, or launching an Apollo Moon Rocket (especially if you were the guy who had the 8% Kingfishers that evening).

After dinner, the Kingfishers, and solving the light switch Rubik's Cube, I was pretty wiped out, and it was time for a peaceful night's sleep.

The next day would be our first full day of riding. Although my confidence was high after Delhi's chaotic roads, there surely would be more surprises. This would prove to be especially true as we went further into India's countryside.

As I woke up in my dark hotel room, it took me a few moments to realize where I was. What took longer was figuring out how to turn on the lights via the Rubik's cube, but mashing all the light switches on the main panel helped me regain my focus and vision in this now dimly lit room. The bigger issue was finding the correct switch for the hot water. So after a short and cold shower (I didn't find the switch), it was time to meet everyone downstairs and get our plan for the day together over some much-needed coffee.

Once downstairs, I looked at each of my friends, then myself in the mirror. It wasn't difficult to tell who consumed the 8% Kingfisher beers the previous evening. I also learned that one of them went back to the store for another beer after I went to sleep, but the store was closed. That didn't stop my highly motivated friend from discovering that there was a guy next to the store selling Kingfishers at a mildly elevated price from a ditch next to the store.

With a few coffees in us, we loaded the motorcycles and we were ready for another day of adventure. Today would be our first full day of riding from Alawar to Jaipur, which was only around 160km. There would be plenty of sights to see along the way as we traveled through some pretty remote backroads, and Google Maps even had us go through a field trail for a few kilometers. We took turns leading, although my cell service was still unreliable, so we would only have me lead when we were on one road for a solid length of time.

After an hour or so, we decided to take a break in a small village and get a few bananas and some water. It only took a couple of minutes before most of the village came out to meet us all. Even a school bus stopped and let the kids off to check out the bikes and talk with us. It reminded me of my first experience in India 20 years prior. This would become a familiar sight for us, with crowds coming up to us to chat and take selfies. They were all the friendliest people. We enjoyed these stops and opportunities to engage with the locals in these little villages that were so far off the map.

Our next stop was to check out a step well. One of the guys had this thing for step wells, and by the end of the trip, I hoped I would never see another step well again. I think he had to have like a Global map for them. Step wells are really just a deep brick hole in the ground with several steps from all angles going down into the hole to fetch water with buckets and bring it back up. Some of them went over 60 feet down.

Once we arrived in Jaipur, it was early afternoon, and the traffic was really starting to become congested. This made it a challenge for me to stay within line of sight of the guys (again). There is a huge fort in Jaipur called Nahargarh Fort. It was the first of many forts we would be visiting. The fort was stunning to walk around, and the views from that high ground were spectacular. We could view the entire city from this fort.

As we wrapped up the tour of the fort and returned to the lower ground, the traffic had become beyond insane. The streets were narrow and filled with tuk tuks, motorcycles, cows, cars and just overall chaos. It seemed every inch that was gained to stay in a tight group was a fight. The other drivers weren't so much aggressive as it was just cramped and tight. My bike got scuffed up by a bus at one turn, but I had to keep on riding to keep up with the others.

By the time we reached our hotel, we were all more than ready for a Kingfisher, and we each hoped they were the 8% ones. We survived another day motorcycling through this fabulous, but intense country and were eagerly looking forward to what the following day would bring.

Waking up the next day was a little bit easier. This was because there were only three switches on the wall. Much simpler than the usual 100+ switches in the previous hotels. In those, I wasn't sure if I was turning on a fan, light, or launching an Apollo mission. I was even able to find the switch for the water heater to have a nice hot shower. After a short walk to obtain some much-needed caffeine and having the Royal Enfield Himalayans loaded, we were ready to head out and kick the day off.

Today was going to be about 250 kilometers of riding to the small town of Bhilwara. Along the way, we would visit one of the very few Jain temples in India. Upon arrival, we instantly noticed the amount of detail on everything. The temple was more than one can comprehend in just a short visit.

We enjoyed soaking in the culture, both from the temple and the locals, who enjoyed taking selfies with us. After a bit, it was time to start moving, as we had one more temple to visit and a 2-hour ride to where we planned to stay for the evening.

The next temple was only about 10 minutes away, but Google routed us through a local bazaar. Thankfully, we didn't attempt anything like this on Day 1 in India, as it would have been more than overwhelming. I figured this would start getting interesting as soon as the streets began to narrow and the crowds filled in. I cannot find a comparison other than to imagine driving through the 2004 Red Sox World Series Celebration at Government Center in Boston. Packed doesn't even begin to describe it. Normally, I would have thought motos weren't supposed to be driving through here, but seeing one or two other motorcycles (other than us), I figured we weren't doing anything too bad.

The ride was tight. We slowly made our way through the crowd with a constant honking and a light nudge of a pedestrian or three until we finally arrived at the temple. We weren't quite swarmed by people looking for selfies, but there were crowds everywhere around us. As always, they were super friendly, so we took our time with each group and chatted with them about where we were from and where we were going.

Once we took a short tour of the temple and were asked for a bunch more selfies, it was time to head back on the road and the path to that road, you guessed it, was through the same bazaar we squeezed through on the way in. By this time, we were familiar with how to negotiate through the crowd, and we did so.

As we approached Bhilwara, we were more than ready to get off the bikes and get some dinner. Well, India had different plans for us. It turns out Bhilwara (as with other small towns, we would learn) requires the hotels to file paperwork with local authorities for foreigners. Normally, this isn't too big a deal, but in this case, none of the hotels in this town had the proper paperwork, nor did they seem too motivated to obtain it. This forced us to drive another hour until we were in a more populated area where we could finally rest for the evening. We were cutting it close with time as the bright red sun was just beginning to set as we pulled into the hotel. This was a fine way to wrap up another day of motorcycling through India.

India: Rolling North

The number of temples and shrines we visited throughout Rajasthan in India had become mind-boggling. They each had their appeal and drew for one crowd or another. It seems as though there was a temple for everyone, and as soon as I began wondering just how far apart and diverse the temples were, we pulled into one that finally fully resonated with all of us. It was the Temple of Om Banna.

This wasn't just any temple. Temple Om Banna is a temple dedicated to fallen motorcycle riders and to provide a blessing and a safe journey for all travelers. As legend has it, in 1988, a motorcyclist lost control of his Royal Enfield here and hit a tree and was instantly killed. His motorcycle ended up in a nearby ditch. The police recovered it and brought it to their station. The following day, the motorcycle was missing from the police station and was rediscovered back where it had originally crashed. This happened several times until the locals declared this a miracle, and the Om Banna Shrine was created.

The Shrine is located right off the highway and is hard to miss with all the food carts, people, and yes, motorcyclists. It is said that travelers who do not stop at this Temple will have bad luck for the continuation of their journey. Not wanting to have any bad luck (and more importantly, to check out this cool temple), we quickly pulled in on our Royal Enfields.

There were probably a couple of hundred people there as we entered the open-air temple. There was incense burning, and just a few meters past that, we could see the Royal Enfield encased in glass with offerings surrounding it. These offerings included food, money, and small liquor bottles (makes sense, right?). The entire scene was surreal. The motorcycle did seem to have a life of its own. I am not sure if it was just from the ambience surrounding it or if it was indeed a miracle we were gazing upon. Either way, the temple was something that we each connected with in our own way and in our own space.

Upon packing up to leave, one of my friends decided he would go ahead of us and get some kilometers in, as he was a faster rider and would find a hotel for us for that evening. The rest of us were in no rush and decided to get off the highway to go slower and take in the countryside. We were all pretty relaxed as another busy day was winding down. It seems that anytime riding in India, as soon as you lower your guard, India feels it and will throw something at you as a reminder to respect your surroundings.

The two of us were on a long straight. My friend was leading as I was gazing outward, and I saw something dart under my friend's moto. Whatever it was, it was for a moment consumed underneath the bike and seemed to have disappeared. By the time this all processed (split seconds), I realized it was a small child who was being called by her sibling on the other side of the road.

The child was underneath the bike from my perspective. My mind quickly raced through about 100 different reactions and emotions. It seems I blinked, and then the child reappeared on the other side of the motorcycle, still running, seemingly oblivious to what had almost happened. Neither of us could fully process how the child wasn't killed or injured in any way. It was just that close.

We both pulled over instantly. My friend needed about 10 minutes and a call to his family back in Canada to calm down and process what had happened, or almost happened. Once we had regained our composure, we began the short and very quiet ride to our hotel, where we met up with our friend. He instantly could tell something was up as we pulled into the hotel. When he asked what was up, the only reply I could say was "Om Banna."

Awakening the following morning (still with some uneasiness from our close encounter the previous day), it took more than one coffee to jar us back into the present and rid the cobwebs from yesterday. We had a full day planned, and although we weren't rushed, we wanted to get moving to ensure we could fit everything in.

Our first stop was a beautiful fort in Jaisalmer. This was an incredible structure from every angle. Forts in Rajasthan all dominate each city's backdrop. While this was an incredible location and area, I had performed some research prior and slyly snuck off and ducked into a small store. The sign said "Govt. Authorized Bhang Shop." In no time, I returned with what looked to the others like a pile of cookies. My friends assumed it was just some Indian bakery and didn't give it any more thought. We took a few photos and then continued on our way further north.

As we continued north, we encountered a nasty patch of construction. The construction dragged on for over an hour. There was nothing but breathing in dust and loose gravel, challenging our ability to remain upright. Upon nearing the end, we stopped for a quick bottle of water, and were relieved to see the highway ramp that would take us about 50 kilometers to our destination to wrap up the day. The entertainment at this stop was a guy who was beyond hammered. He could barely stand, much less form any sort of sentence (in English or Hindi). We did our best to ignore him before saddling up and making our way toward the highway.

As we approached the entry gate to the highway, the person controlling the gate wasn't going to let us on, and I knew right away this was one of those highways where motos were not allowed. Instantly, the thought of having to return for another hour of riding through construction popped into my head, and I could see the same feeling wash over my friends' faces as well. Just as we were about to concede, who comes stumbling up but the drunk from the rest stop, more animated than ever. He nudged the toll worker aside and raised the gate himself for us to pass under. Just like that, we were on our way.

We were each pretty happy to not be revisiting that construction mess, and the highway conditions were pristine. There was minimal traffic on the new pavement. Life was good, obviously too good, and I knew that somewhere between our current location and the 50 kilometers we had remaining that we would be paying for this one way or another. I noticed the other vehicles looking intently at us, and of course, there were no other motos on the highway.

The 50 kilometers went by fast, and as we took our exit, we saw another gate that was closed and a couple of people coming out to "greet" us. They spoke no English, but it was clear they wanted us to turn around. Turning around made no sense to any of us. It was like doing the same violation, but twice. After we took turns with our failed attempts to get them to raise the gate (and with turning around a hard no for a solution), we spotted a sidewalk with no gate. This would be our new exit.

We quickly took the initiative to exit the highway using the sidewalk. The workers were chasing us with pens and paper in a failed attempt to write our license tag numbers down. What we did sounds a bit dodgy, but I solely blame it on the drunk guy who originally raised the gate. Either way, we made great time, had a story, and to the best of my knowledge, none of us got in any trouble for it. We needed that extra time as it was late in the day and we still had one more Temple to visit: The Rat Temple.

After ensuring we didn't have any tails on us from our highway escapades, it was a short turnaround at the hotel before a visit to a temple in Deshnoke. I had heard much about this temple over the years and really wasn't sure what to expect. What was the urban legend, and what was actually the truth surrounding this strange place? This temple was named the Karni Mata Temple, or as it is better known, the Rat Temple.

Well, it turns out this temple is everything I imagined it would be, but actually experiencing it was something that none of us were prepared for. Karni Mata is a Hindu Temple that believes rats are the reincarnated souls of a local storyteller family that died during a famine. The rats are everywhere. There are just thousands all over, and they are fed quite well. There are even several troughs for them to eat out of, and donations of grains and milk are frequently left to appease these local deities.

To add to the cringe factor, you must remove your shoes to enter the temple. As we removed our shoes and began our walk down the long hallways, out of the corner of my eye, I would see things scurrying from left to right, and then right to left, and then just everywhere. After entering the temple, there are several long hallways with raised troughs that the rats climb up to eat grains and seeds. Every corner we cautiously walked around, we would see more and more rats. Surreal doesn't begin to describe the place. The rats are so well fed, however, that when walking around the other parts of the city, there wasn't a rat to be seen. It seems they all stay in the temple. With such an abundance of food, why not? This didn't help us get to sleep any easier, though, as our hotel was across the street from the temple.

We weren't getting nearly as much sleep as we wanted (due to the temple's proximity), and we were anxious to get out of town and put as many kilometers between us and the rats as possible. Nonetheless, the temple was an experience to be had that few people get the opportunity to embrace.

Our next stop would be Amritsar, including a special trip to the Pakistan/India Border Closing Ceremony and the famous Golden Palace. This would prove to be one of our more adventurous days in India, in more ways than one.

India: Amritsar

Shaking off the continual feeling of being around rats, we began a 4-hour drive to Amritsar. It was crucial that we get there early, as our plan was to Uber 45 minutes to the Pakistani Indian border for the closing ceremony. From what I had heard, it was just an insane spectacle to witness. Our ride was almost uneventful this day. Almost.

Around 10:00 a.m., we were still within the state of Rajasthan, and we pulled over in a bustling city for a coffee break. It didn't take too long before we were surrounded by locals wanting selfies with us and asking a lot of questions. This was mostly normal for us, although it did seem at this particular stop, there was an alarming number of people surrounding us (not just the usual five or so). Within a few minutes, three serious-looking men sat at our table and began asking some deeper questions than the normal chit-chat. They asked to see our passports and stated they were Indian Federal Police. I replied with "Show me yours first." Which they did. Okay. It seems we were in a tourist forbidden zone as we were just a few kilometers from the Pakistani Border. In Rajasthan was not a good thing (in Amritsar, this was a non-issue).

Not wanting to lose physical control of our passports, we chatted them up and, in unison, began to de-escalate the situation. This took about 10 minutes of back and forth as two more Federal Authorities joined in the questioning. There had been no signs or warnings stating this was a non-tourist area. I guess it was just common knowledge to most (the common knowledge we lacked). Eventually, the situation worked itself out. They offered to buy us another coffee, but we thought it best to continue to Amritsar and not test our luck any further. We mounted our Royal Enfields and were on our way.

Shortly after we arrived in Amritsar without any further issues, we parked the bikes and paged an Uber to go to the Pakistani Border. Along the ride, I sat in the front seat and began eating my "baked goods" from the Bhang shop that I had purchased two days ago. I was talking to the Uber driver about pretty much everything under the sun while wolfing down my Bhang pastry. My endless banter helped pass the time until we pulled into the parking garage and began our short walk to what looked like a giant stadium.

There were thousands of Indians entering the long tunnel to the stadium interior. The really cool thing about this experience is that, as foreigners, we were treated as VIPs and given the best seats in the house. We were only 10 meters from the Pakistan border. This was after three different security and passport checks. Once we were seated, we noticed it would be more than an hour before the ceremony started, but that made no difference to those on the India side, as music was thumping through the speakers. People were selling popcorn, sodas, Indian Flags, and all kinds of souvenirs. It was like being at Fenway Park but with much more going on in every direction.

As the time drew near for the ceremony, we could see through the fence that the Pakistani side was filling up. They had their own music thumping. Meanwhile, on the India side, there was a "ring announcer" riling up all those on our side to include hundreds, in a massive mosh pit on the stadium floor.

While these pre-ceremony festivities were occurring, my friend commented on how my eyes seemed a bit...well, off, and he noticed I was acting a bit freaked out. He nudged me to ask what I thought of the show. I could barely reply. After a bit, I finally answered, saying, "There sure is a lot going on here."

It took a bit before I finally let him in on what was going on. The Bhang shop pastries were a type of legal edible marijuana, and I guess I had consumed a rather large portion during the Uber ride in. I was higher than a cat on acid at the India/Pakistan border, while all these activities were occurring around me. Oh, man, it was a hell of a show. It was probably the craziest thing I have ever witnessed. Each stadium grew louder and louder. The only analogy I have is this: Picture Gillette Stadium cut in half with two football games going on simultaneously, and being on the 50-yard line.

Fortunately for me, once the actual border ceremony began, the ambiance began to tame down somewhat as the soldiers each performed their border closing duties (to include a halftime moment of them shaking hands with a short bow to one another). The flags of each country were lowered, carefully folded, and the ceremony came to a close. My eyes were about as wide as you can imagine throughout it all. We made our way back to the Uber for a relaxing 45-minute ride back to our hotel. The day was far from over though, as we were to have dinner at the Golden Palace that evening.

As we arrived back in Amritsar, my eyes were returning to almost normal from my Bhang border journey that had still left me speechless. We were all still in awe of the entire border scene, but we would have time to reflect on it later. Now we had to walk about two kilometers from our hotel to the Golden Palace and experience having dinner there. It wasn't quite like anything we expected.

As we entered the grounds of the Golden Temple, we had to check our shoes at the gate and place a hat on our heads to adhere to the Temple's dress code. The temple and surrounding buildings were so lit up (not as lit up as I was at the Pakistani Border, but lit up nonetheless). We walked around the inner walls of this magnificent building and eventually made our way to what seemed to be a huge dining hall. We learned that this temple provides free food to 100,000 people every day! It is the single largest free kitchen in the world.

Once in the dining hall, we were given a metal tray, some utensils, and a cup. We followed the people in front of us into an even larger room where there were just rows and rows of people sitting down on the floor, eating and drinking. After we sat down, it was only a few moments before a server came by with a giant ladle and plopped some food onto our tray. A few servers were dishing out rice, water, bread, and a sauce. For the number of people there, this setup was extremely efficient, to the point that once we were finished with our first portion, seconds were just a few moments away. The food was very satisfying, and by the time we each had consumed two or three servings, we were set to get up and drop our trays and utensils off at the dishwasher counter.

After dinner, we spent about an hour or so just admiring the beauty of this massive architectural structure. It was quite a sight, and it was one of those places that really had its own pulse. The temple had a presence you could feel.

It was quite an eventful day in Amritsar. We retired to our rooms to get some sleep and prepare for the next day's adventure.

India: Amritsar to Rishikesh

Loading the bikes the following morning, we were still basking in the Golden Temple's magical glow. We were amped up for our next leg. This portion would be a relaxing two-day journey via Shimla to Rishikesh and would give us a glimpse of the lower Himalayan Mountain ranges. The roads would mostly be mountain twisties. This was what we wanted for riding (or so we thought).

The roads, although having great twisties, were extremely narrow. So narrow, in fact, that on more than one occasion, oncoming buses would find themselves in stalemates as to who would back down and reverse to allow the other to pass. When this happened, we usually could squeeze through while they were conferring on who would back up. There were also the usual obstructions: Monkeys, cows, goats, and an occasional camel. This made for very slow going, and by the end of this portion of the trip, we were starting to miss the major roads we had previously ridden.

A sure way to tell you are off the beaten path is when you have to refuel your bike by purchasing fuel that is brought to you in plastic water bottles. Along these roads, this refueling process became the norm, which I always find cool.

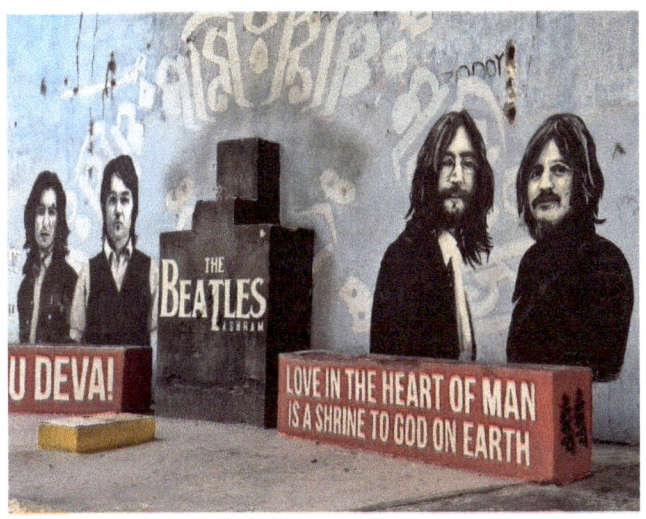

All in all, it was part of the journey and we had a blast on this portion of our ride. Upon arriving in Rishikesh and seeing the Ganges River, we were exhausted and looking forward to a few days off to explore the city and have a couple of cold Kingfisher beers. I think I may have consumed another Bhang pastry as well.

The only thing I knew of Rishikesh was that the Beatles wrote most of their White Album there. We did the tourist thing and visited the Beatles' Ashram (where they stayed during that period). The Ashram was mostly overrun by jungle, but it was a decent side quest and a reason to listen to the White Album that evening.

We took a different way back to our hotel from the Beatles' Ashram. It allowed us to cross a narrow (mostly pedestrian) suspension bridge over the Ganges. We were about 100 feet above the river on this narrow, bouncy bridge, moving very slowly due to the immense pedestrian traffic. It allowed us to observe Rishikesh from our high location, including the ceremonial burning of bodies along the Ganges' banks. The crossing took about five minutes, but there was so much to take in during that five minutes that it felt as though we were on the bridge for hours. It was other-worldly, to say the least.

After reaching the other side of the bridge, we parked the motos. We sat along the Ganges and took everything in. Rishikesh was where we would begin to part ways on this journey, as my friends needed to return to Canada, their jobs, their wives, their children, and their world.

It was a crossroads for me. I didn't have a next location or activity planned, as the trip through India during the past month had consumed every waking hour. I wasn't too concerned; this was the norm for me, and I knew I would figure it out. I just didn't expect to learn of my next destination by a massive thunderstorm awakening me and prompting me to check my phone. Upon seeing a barrage of missed calls and messages I learned that sadly The United States of America was my next destination.

Travel Stories

Racing the Sun

Finding myself in Arizona in the winter months has become my norm. Arizona provides one of the better climates for riding and camping, and I can camp there without waking up next to a frozen Gatorade bottle in my tent (this happens way too often to me).

Over the past three years, wintering here, I had missed one of the more moving Veterans Day memorials, the Anthem Veterans Memorial in Anthem, Arizona. This fascinating tribute to our country's Soldiers, Airmen, Marines, Sailors, and Coast Guard (no Space Force yet) is located just two minutes off Interstate 17.

I visited the Veterans Memorial on several occasions while stopping at the Starbucks in Anthem (insert BMW GS joke here) before riding to work in Phoenix or Tucson. What makes the Anthem Veterans Memorial so special is that on November 11th at 11:11, the sun aligns with the Memorial and shines directly through its five pillars (each pillar represents a branch of the military), that lights the Great Seal of the United States of America. The pillar heights correspond with the number of people in each branch (Army, Navy, Air Force, Marines, and Coast Guard).

This year, when I rode my GS to Phoenix for routine maintenance, I saw the sign on I-17 for the Memorial. I looked down, and it was 11:08. I had a chance to make it! Pulling in my clutch and clicking down two gears brought me to this new destination. It was exhilarating! I was literally racing the sun to be where I needed to be at 11:11.

I didn't make it in time. Only five minutes or so had passed, but the eclipse of the Great Seal was not in totality anymore. That is how accurate this modern-day sundial is. The radiant glow from it was still vibrant, and even though it wasn't fully in totality, it was still very impressive.

Many people surrounded the Memorial on this day, and just as many rode motorcycles here as a Veterans Day Pilgrimage. It is always a great day whenever I chat with Veterans, especially at such an impressive monument on Veterans Day.

Having been so close to seeing this Memorial at its peak has placed it on my 2023 list. I will join other Veterans riding to the Memorial and the festivities on this special day in the future and ensure Starbucks will be part of the experience to meet my BMW GS ownership obligations.

Toad Rock Campground, British Columbia

When traveling I keep a loose schedule. I talk to people along my journey and gain insight on what is best to see, and just as importantly, what is best to avoid. In 2017, while sitting outside Starbucks somewhere in Washington state, a couple asked where I was headed (I ride a GS1200; frequenting Starbucks is an ownership obligation). I didn't have much of a destination in mind, and the couple asked if I had my passport, which I did. They recommended visiting Toad Rock Campground in British Columbia. Just like that, Toad Rock Campground became my weekend destination.

I entered Canada through Idaho. It always seems that once crossing the border, everything becomes more magnificent. Trees are larger, there is more wildlife, the mountains are higher, the water is bluer, you get the point. I crossed the Canadian border at Rykerts, B.C. This was a bit out of the way, but it was what the couple had recommended. The main reason (besides 3A being a phenomenal road) was that I would take the World's Longest Free Ferry across Kootenay Lake to Balfour. Once I disembarked the ferry in Balfour, it was just a short hop to Toad Rock. It turns out taking the longer route was absolutely the right call.

Arriving at Toad Rock, I dismounted from the GS and went to check in. The lady running the camp stated it was full, but I could find a patch of grass in the back and set up camp. I signed in and paid (I want to say $10 CDN, but don't fully remember). She then looked at me, pointed and said, "If you're an asshole, I will throw your ass OUT!" To that I swiftly replied, "Yes, Ma'am." Later, I found out she even makes motorcycle clubs remove their vests and colors to avoid any friction within the camp. This was all fine with me.

I rode to the back forty to find my piece of lawn. My area was located outside the wooded main area. The camp looked really cool with lights hung all through it to include a central gazebo with a stage, bar, and a very large refrigerator, which was firmly held closed by a bungee cord. I asked someone what the deal was with this cord. They replied that there was a large pig that wandered the campground to scare the bears away, and if you don't bungee the refrigerator, the pig will open the door and drink all your beer. Interesting indeed.

My camp was set up by 13:00, and I discovered a local loop for an afternoon blast around southern B.C. The loop entailed riding Route 31 around to Route 6. From Route 6, I dropped down into Nelson, B.C. Nelson would make a great stopping point for a late lunch and has a quaint downtown area to walk around and stretch. The roads were in great shape and outside the mountain views were being minimized from several wildfires it was a perfect June day to enjoy this part of the province. What made the day even better was stopping twice to jump into an ice-cold mountain stream that hugged the road to cool off. The streams were cold and refreshing, especially after riding in full gear during the peak of the day.

Upon leaving the streams, my entire body would be tingling (like I just ate a piece of peppermint gum) from the extreme change in temperature it had just experienced. Having been fully refreshed from my swims, it was time to eat. My stomach was growling for a burger just as I entered the town of Nelson. While eating a giant bacon burger and enjoying a cold Kokanee beer, I suddenly heard a loud chopping through the air. I recognized that sound from years before. It was a Chinook helicopter coming to refill its water bucket in the lake to continue fighting the wildfires. Once that show was over and my burger was finished, it was time to head back to Toad Rock and see what was going on at camp for entertainment. I would not be disappointed.

As I arrived at camp around 17:00, the pavilion in the middle was just getting warmed up with people piling in, serving drinks from the BYOB bar, retrieving beers from the refrigerator (and remembering to secure the beers from the thirsty pig). It wasn't long before riders were randomly grabbing musical instruments to play. Everyone was welcoming as they took turns sharing their motorcycle adventure stories.

At this point, I realized we all were in the middle of a great motorcycle story, just living here in the present moment. The festivities continued late into the night. As the night wore on and people slowly began to drift off to their campsites, I decided it was time to return to my tent too. The only problem was that I couldn't find my campsite. I knew it was in the lawn section, but that seemed impossible to find as I went by the same tents a few times as I wearily followed the colored lights strung throughout the trees. I began to worry that I'd have to locate the owner to ground guide me back to my campsite. Does meandering the campground hopelessly lost constitute being an asshole? It was at this moment that I saw a familiar landmark that marked my tent location, and I haphazardly slid into my home for the evening. This was a day that fully encompassed what being a motorcyclist is all about: Living in the present, embracing each moment, and bonding with fellow riders.

Charlie Don't Paddleboard:
A Baja New Year's Story

There was no better way to ring in 2023 than camping off my motorcycle on a beautiful beach in Bahia Conception in Baja, Mexico. The only thing that made the moment more special was a nice Cuban cigar, Tecates, and Tequila with my new friends in the palapas to my left and right, while sitting around a fire. Somehow, I managed to make it until 10:00 p.m., that is equal to a Boston New Year, and I surpassed my previous Baja New Year by 1 hour. I was pretty proud of myself.

Groggily awaking the next morning to the sunrise peering over the mountains across the bay was a serene way to start the New Year. Once I had a coffee (or three) in me, I decided to pack up and make my way back north. The plan was originally to hotel in Guerrero Negro for the night, but I had made such incredible time riding that I arrived in town by 11:30, and it seemed too early to stop for the day. The biggest problem with this is once you leave Guerrero Negro there isn't much (really anything) until you arrive in Gonzaga Bay. That destination is another 4+ hours of riding and the possibility of bad winds. I rolled the dice and decided to attempt the ride to Gonzaga, confident I would arrive just before sunset. I had confirmed sunset was at 16:49 PST.

The ride up was rather uneventful, and even the winds seemed to be cooperating with me on the last leg of this ride. In pulling up to the Rancho Grande Tienda to reserve a campsite, refuel the bike, and load up on firewood, I were starting to feel the 320 miles I had just completed. One of the cool things about camping in this location is the rather long bundle of firewood they provide. Every time I load the wood on the moto, it looks like some biplane. What completes the biplane feeling is riding to the palapas on the bay; you are parallel with an airstrip, so you actually feel like you are about to take off. Just as I hit the 1-kilometer dirt road, the winds began to increase heavily. This was the norm for this part of Baja and wasn't too alarming for me.

Thankfully, the palapa provided me with some protection from the swirling gusts, but not from the roaring freight train sounds that would keep me awake through the night as a demoralizing reminder that I'll have to ride through them the following day.

After setting up my home for the evening, it was time for a cold Tecate beer to unwind and enjoy the gorgeous views of the bay and the mountains that surround it. As I sat in my chair, I noticed a lone paddleboarder and became a bit alarmed by his lack of movement while he struggled to fight the wind to return to shore. He was quite a ways out, and it was obvious the wind was physically and mentally wearing him down from this difficult battle. I could see him stand up to paddle ferociously for a few moments, and then he would lie on the board to rest. This went on for about one more Tecate when I noticed it was 15:45. People were beginning to gather on the shore to watch his valiant yet seemingly unsuccessful attempt to return to his camp, but he wasn't getting any closer. It was time for me to walk the beach and see who this person was with, gain insight on his experience level, how long he was out for, and determine next steps (if any were needed).

After a few minutes, I found his wife, who didn't seem to be concerned until I mentioned that sunset would be in an hour. At that moment, the full weight of the situation set in, and she became frantic. Being one to always travel with a SpotGen 3 GPS emergency beacon, I powered it on, gave her a brief tutorial on how to activate the SOS button, handed it to her and said, "If I am not back in 15 minutes, you push the SOS button." I then directed her to drive the bay in search of a fisherman or boater who could assist. While she was working the problem from that angle, I fired up the BMW GS1200 and returned to the tienda to see if I could find a local that could assist in what clearly was becoming a rescue operation.

The locals in the tienda didn't seem to know anyone who could help. This was not what I expected, and my brain was scrambling for any other ideas to save this person. As I exited the store, the man's wife came flying into the parking lot, creating a mini dust storm from her sprinter van. She was even more panicked than earlier. Just as I was about to take the GPS beacon, return to the location of the paddle boarder and press SOS, we saw a 1960s VW van with some surfers with their boards on the roof. After explaining the situation, they fully agreed to help, and we all raced back to the beach. We had 40 minutes of sun left before it disappeared over the desert mountains behind us. Once our rescue caravan arrived, one of the surfers quickly donned his wetsuit, grabbed his board, and was off into the cold, windy waters. Fortunately, it didn't take him very long to reach the distressed paddler, secure his paddleboard to his surfboard and tow him back in. Everyone was safe and back on shore with 10 minutes of sunlight remaining.

The rescue operation was a success. The hero surfers made a hasty exit just as the last rays of light from the sun began to fade into the lonely desert. An hour later, the family came over to my palapa to gift me with a couple of bottles of wine as a thank you for assisting in the rescue mission. Of course, I invited them to share my campfire. Chatting with the paddleboarder, I learned this was his first paddleboarding experience. Together, we relived the moments of the day from each of our perspectives while drinking the wine and enjoying the glow of the fire. What could have been a much worse ending was nothing more than a valuable lesson for him. The true heroes were the surfers, and I never even got their names before they rolled back down the dusty road and into the Baja desert.

Paddle Boarding Horseshoe Bend

Since my last story was on paddleboarding, I thought sticking with the topic would be a great opportunity to share a unique and exciting experience. Camping off a paddleboard at the base of Horseshoe Bend in Page, Arizona. This was to be a 2-day, 15-mile trip down the Colorado River from Glenn Canyon Dam to Lee's Ferry and would include one night of camping off our paddleboards. As an avid motorcycle camper, I thought camping off a paddleboard would be right up my alley, as the amount of gear from a moto to a paddleboard was relatively the same. This adventure would bring me to one of the most hostile environments in the United States, all while living it from a new perspective, being on top of the frigid waters of the Colorado River.

The adventure began with camping near Page, Arizona, and a day of light paddleboarding on Lake Powell to gain more familiarity and confidence on the board. This was more for myself, as the two friends I was traveling with were both very experienced paddlers. My paddling was limited to a couple of 8-mile runs on the Salt River near Phoenix and a horrible, windy day off the Colorado River, where I launched from Hoover Dam. The Salt River had portions of minor rapids, but the environment was much tamer than we would experience along the Colorado River.

The Colorado River water is extremely cold even during the spring. Contrasting the freezing water was the ambient air temperatures that reached the high 90s (with no place to find shade or relief from the sun above the golden canyon walls that surrounded us). Adding to the natural environmental threats, there can be winds that blow up the river so strongly that you cannot paddle against them, even when going downriver. A year prior, we were supposed to do a camping trip and ended up having to do an 18-mile paddle in heavy winds; on that trip, we were not able to camp as the winds were forecast to be worse the next day. I didn't want to put myself through that again. That night, we made our way to Horseshoe Bend in our car to watch the sunset and look down over the edge to see where we would camp the next evening.

The day we were set to launch, the winds were calm. At 8:00 a.m., we loaded our watercraft onto a powerboat at Lee's Ferry that would deliver us to the base of Glen Dam. It was a cold ride in the boat to our drop-off location as the sun was still hidden behind the massive walls that went straight up nearly a thousand feet. Every bend we went around, I was in constant awe. It was as if every element that you can face in nature was in full view for us to admire, respect, and fear. Once dropped off, we unloaded our gear, and took a few minutes to gain our composure before starting our 15-mile journey downriver.

Pushing our boards off the shoreline, it was still cold, and between the 40-degree water and 50-degree air, none of us wanted to stand up on the boards. Making a small error that could cause us to capsize during this delicate time would result in hypothermia with little hope of warming up until the sun crested above the canyon walls more than two hours later. The winds were absent, and with an occasional dam release, we just coasted down the river effortlessly. Having no headwinds was so much more pleasant than our previous time on this fully exposed river when we spent the day battling a constant headwind.

When the sun finally glimpsed above the canyon walls, they instantly lit up forming a beautiful golden prison. We we were trapped in this prison with neon aqua waters. Waters so clear you can see fish swimming 20 feet below your board. We had dispersed the weight of our gear between the three boards and then balanced them out as best we could. We even had a bundle of firewood secured with Rok Straps for what we hoped would be a magical night under the stars. Along the way, we stopped occasionally for a snack, a beer, or a short hike. There are some hidden petroglyphs along the river where you can disembark from your board and hike in to view them. This made for a perfect, slow-paced and enjoyable day that we all fully embraced.

It was still early, yet due to the lack of headwinds and numerous dam releases, we were already arriving at our camp at Mile 9. Mile 9 camp is at the turn of Horseshoe Bend. What made this really cool wasn't the view (it all looked really the same with giant canyon walls on both sides of you). What made this special was that when you looked up the thousand-foot walls, you could see hundreds of tourists looking down at you and waving. I felt like we were in a zoo exhibit. We set up camp and spent a relaxing afternoon swimming, chatting with other boaters (mostly kayakers and fellow paddlers), and just enjoying the fact that we weren't battling winds. This was quite a rewarding day.

After a perfect day of mild paddling, relaxing and gazing off into this beautiful yet intimidating environment, the day slowly turned into evening. It wasn't long before we started a campfire. Sitting around a campfire with new friends, cold beers from our Ice Mule Cooler, and exchanging stories is always the high point of my day. I wandered off to use the bathroom when I noticed flashing from above. At first, I thought it was the stars beginning to peer from above the cliffs, but it wasn't. The flashes I saw were the tourists above using their phones and flashlights to signal "hello" down to us. As I zipped my pants up, I already had the "It was the cold water that caused shrinkage" or the "You're 1,000 feet away…of course it looks smaller". For some reason, my new friends around the campfire didn't understand my humor, and the stories continued until the flashes from the tourists above faded about the same time we did.

Having slept great that night at the base of one of the most iconic photo spots in the United States, it was now time to pack up. Winds always seemed to gain intensity as the day wore on, so we wanted an early start to avoid this threat, but there were no winds on this day, either. It was almost as if the river was rewarding us for having passed its initiation from that previous windy trip that didn't allow camping. The river was so calm that we were able to even lie down on our paddleboards and allow the current and dam releases to carry us the remaining 6 miles downriver without any effort. This is how paddleboarding should be, but I knew this was an anomaly on the Colorado River. In my experience, tailwinds are like unicorns. They really don't exist, yet somehow this trip we were surrounded by a herd of unicorns.

It wasn't long before we could see Lee's Ferry ahead of us on the right. We made it to shore and began the process of packing our gear up to return to Lake Powell for one more night of camping before returning to southern Arizona. Since paddleboarding Horseshoe Bend, anytime I see pictures of this location, I zoom in and can often see paddleboards, kayaks, and tents at the beach when everyone else is just looking at the full view of the photo. I absolutely prefer my new perspective of this part of Glenn Canyon National Recreation Area, through my eyes of a paddleboarder.

Wildlife in the Southwest: Javelina

Having grown up in Maine, I spent most of my childhood experiencing life up close with nature. I have always been drawn to unique wildlife in different regions of our country. In the Southwest, this is especially true as the terrain is so different from Maine, or really anywhere else I have traveled. Many people think of desert and cactus, sand, maybe an old cow skull on a fence post and envision a region void of life. This couldn't be further from the truth. Once you get out exploring this fragile ecosystem, it's easy to see and hear how much life there is in this harsh environment.

One of the coolest animals I have seen along my travels is the javelina. These beady eyed little critters look very similar to boars or wild pigs but are actually in the rodent family. If you are in the desert during a full moon and the wind is just right, and if you are lucky, you can hear a pack of these little guys chomping up prickly pear cactus and tearing up people's lawns. They are a little local gang of hoodlums causing mischief throughout the neighborhood. Then they disappear into the thick desert underbrush as quickly as they appeared from it.

The first time I saw javelina was while camping along the Arizona and Mexican border. Sleeping in a tiny one person tent, I woke up to what I thought were wild horses munching on some leaves. The sound got louder and closer as whatever it was moved in on my position. I wasn't quite sure what to do, but I wanted to be certain I wasn't trampled by horses in my tent (that's one way to end the story). I popped out of my tent and flicked on my flashlight. What I saw was about 10 pairs of beady little eyes staring back at me and snouts wiggling in all directions. Not having any idea what these things were and not being armed, I began shouting at them, "Quit screwing around!" Little did I know that was the exact command they understood and followed. After a few moments of a harrowing standoff, they took the hint and went around my tent without missing one leaf. The strange looking beasts made their way into the rugged desert terrain as I stood outside my tent, still trying to figure out what had just marched through my campsite.

Frequently wintering in the southwest, I am now very accustomed to these little troublemakers, and it always brings me great joy to see them marching across the street like the Beatles on the Abbey Road Album cover. On more than one occasion, when I see them in the backyard, I will close the gate and jokingly say, "We got us a petting zoo!" In my experience, the javelina are pretty focused on obtaining food and don't pay much attention to us humans being near them. The exception is if you move quickly, make loud noises, or they have babies in their herd.

So, whether these little Star Wars looking creatures are hanging out around my campsite in the middle of the desert or foraging through the neighbors' yards, they are a pleasant reminder that the environments I travel through change in many ways. The javelina are a vital part of the desert's fragile ecosystem that we are guests in to enjoy and embrace.

Disclaimer: Opening a javelina petting zoo is a foolish thing to do. Do not attempt to pet, embrace, or feed them, as they can turn on you and attack.

Me for VP

To preface this, I am not too much of a political person. For me, the current political scene is an ongoing series of Melrose Place episodes that play out in the background as entertainment. I really don't give it too much thought otherwise. For others, it seems to be deeply rooted in them to be for one side or the other. At times they switch sides, like when Macho Man became a bad guy in the WWF. At any rate, I wanted to state that before this write-up. Enjoy!

In 2016, I found myself dating a girl I had met on Day 1 in boot camp at Fort Jackson, SC. Soldiers were still segregated then between male and female, except on KP. We hit it off and dated for a bit in Fort Gordon, GA, as we were both communication specialists. That faded as I was shipped off to Korea for a year, and we lost contact. Fast forward 23 years or so, and we happened to reconnect when we were both living in Seattle. I was working remotely, and she was quite high up in Seattle's city government. She was very politically active (as you can imagine, being in Seattle). That was fine, and I didn't give it much notice or bother, and I was always well behaved at dinners with the mayor and the other work functions I tagged along on.

It didn't take long for her to start pushing me to take my career more seriously and move from being a project manager to higher management positions. The push wasn't a bad thing from her perspective, I am sure, but I was content where I was. I was great at my job, I could travel, and I had a great team (both on my projects and with my managers).

This didn't stop her from mentioning at every dinner with friends about her wanting me to take my career to the next level. The nagging didn't end. Quite often, when I am being pushed to do something I really don't want to, I either dig my heels in and refuse or… I go FULL into it so obnoxiously that the point comes across pretty clearly as to where I stand. Even as a child, if I got in trouble at school (a daily occurrence), my Mom would make me bring wood up from the basement, and to protest this more than once, I would bring up so much, and stack it so high, that they would need a step ladder to use the top pieces. For good or bad, my mentality hasn't changed much over the years, and with the girlfriend and her crew constantly nagging me about my career, it was time to take action and put this to bed.

It was a Friday evening in 2016, and we had a group of her city workers and their spouses over for dinner. As the conversation drizzled on, I was waiting for my moment. As she was telling one of her friends how well I had been behaving the past week, I decided it was time. I took a knife and softly dinged my wine glass. "I have some big news, guys. I have formally applied for an upper management position. Actually, a VP position, and I feel I have a great chance here, and this can really boost my career." Everyone was happy, even a few claps ensued. I was then asked what company this VP position was in. I proudly slammed the write-up below on the table while loudly saying, "VP OF THE UNITED STATES OF AMERICA, BABY!!"

Dear Sir, I would like to apply to be your Vice President in 2024. I am a highly motivated individual with valued skills both in leadership and management, which will enable us to lead this country as it has never been led before. My skills have been honed beginning in my youth as a soldier with the 82nd Airborne Division. These skills have only grown throughout my life as a successful graduate of Boston University and as a leader in the field of project management. Thank you for your consideration, and I look forward to working with you to make America great again.

Sincerely,

Michael Huber, PMP

Well, as you can imagine, that announcement went over like a fart in church. Nonetheless, I stuck with it and doubled down, asking if any of them had applied for the VP position. Of course, none had, so I made it very clear that I now had a better shot than any of them. Needless to say, I got the reaction I was looking for, and my career aspirations were never discussed again. I accomplished my objective.

DONALD J. TRUMP

Thank you for writing to President Donald J. Trump. We are carefully reviewing your message.

President Trump believes the strength of our country lies in the spirit of the American people and their willingness to stay informed and get involved.

He appreciates your taking the time to share your thoughts and sends his best wishes to you and your family.

In 2024, I find myself without a job, so I formally applied yet again and, so far, I have only received the reply you see above. My Dad says I will have to return and work from Washington D.C. if offered the position. I believe as VP I can work remotely (I will negotiate that once I am formally offered the position). I am expecting either an offer letter in the mail or a phone call in the next week or so. I will keep you in the loop on how this new career path works out.

Mount Rainier

Mount Rainier, a two-hour drive south of Seattle, was something I became obsessed with while living in the Pacific Northwest. I loved looking at that volcano. Mount Rainier often wasn't visible during the winter months due to the cloud cover, but when it was visible, it was a sight to be seen, especially at sunset. The entire volcano would glow orange, almost as if it were a 14,000-foot candle. It was magical.

To reach this summit, one has to be extremely skilled as a mountaineer or have a guide due to the multiple avalanches. This was something I had to experience up close, but I didn't have the climbing talent so would have to find another way to experience this.

The following August, I began training by spending two months climbing numerous peaks in Washington until my body felt solid enough for an attempt to climb to Mount Rainier's base camp, Camp Muir. I drove to the base of Mount Rainier in Paradise, Washington, and slept in the back of my car that night. That gave me a better chance of snagging a camp permit for Camp Muir in the morning. This mountain base camp was mostly for those who dared to climb this volcano, and it was nothing more than a hostel at 10,000 feet. It was a small wooden shed with two levels of plywood that held 12 hikers.

The hike up to the camp was a smoker. I left at 7:00 a.m. and didn't reach Camp Muir until 14:00. It was like climbing up a black diamond ski slope. I didn't have crampons, and my pack was quite heavy as I had loaded it with a lot of water (a rookie mistake). Once arriving at the camp and securing a spot in the shed, I spent the rest of the day talking with those who would be summiting in the early hours of the following morning. The climbers begin at night to avoid warmer periods of the day when avalanches are more prevalent.

The hikers all woke around 2:00 a.m. to begin their attempt. Even though the temperatures were low, I decided to get up and see them all leave. This provided me the opportunity to view all the stars and the entire Milky Way spread across an otherwise black night sky. As the hikers made their way, I could hear the loud cracking of avalanches in the distance. Camp Muir was angled so it was well protected, but that loud thunderous sound sure got the hairs on the back of my neck up.

In the morning, as the sun came up, I could see 270 degrees around me, and volcanoes were visible in every direction. It was a sight to behold as I finished my breakfast (the remainder of a crushed Subway sandwich). It was time to begin my descent. The coolest part of this hike was going back down. I brought a large black garbage bag with me on this hike. The reason is that as you descend, there are luges carved throughout the path down the mountain. This allowed the opportunity to glissade, sometimes picking up an unreal amount of speed to the point where I would use my legs as brakes to ensure I didn't get too out of control.

Once returning to a much lower elevation, the snow began to disappear, and it was time to pack the garbage bag up and hike the remaining 2 miles down. Not having slept much the night prior due to the higher elevation, I was looking forward to hitting a breakfast place in Paradise to refuel with something more than the crushed Subway sandwich. I could tell I was close to the base as the people I ran across were less and less in shape or prepared. Once I saw a family wearing Crocs, I knew my breakfast had to be within a ¼ mile or less.

As I entered the café, I got a coffee and a breakfast sandwich. I felt fulfilled because I was able to experience the hike even without summiting. The hike to Camp Muir was still challenging, and I knew it would leave me sore for the next few days. It would also provide memories that have lasted with me. Every time I see Mount Rainier in the Pacific Northwest, I am able to relive my experience and appreciate that magnificent mountain in a more personal way.

El Condor Comida

Pinnacles National Park is the 50th National Park I visited. I believe there are 63 National Parks total (National Park Service keeps adding them yearly, so…). As with all the parks, it is rare to be disappointed with a visit to any of them. In fact, I have visited some of the parks numerous times just to be sure to fully embrace each part of them, as many are quite large.

Pinnacles National Park is one of the lesser visited National Parks. I find this refreshing since there are fewer tourists than in other National Parks, like Yellowstone and Yosemite, where the crowds can be almost overwhelming and detract from the experience. For Pinnacles, I had reserved two nights camping, so once I arrived late in the day, I could knock out a shorter hike and complete a long hike on the spare day. The longer hike I chose was to summit the highest peak in the park, Chalone Peak. The peak reaches 3,304 feet in elevation. That isn't that bad because there is only a 2,034-foot elevation gain from the base. This is a 9 mile trail that snakes through beautiful hills. Every turn provided an incredible panoramic view of the fields below and the mountains that stretched to the sky.

Once summiting the peak, it was time to rehydrate and fuel up with lunch for the hike back. As I sat down, I heard what sounded like someone vomiting. Looking to my left, I saw I was sitting about 25 feet from a California condor. It was tagged with No. 89. The National Park Service tags these rare birds to track and follow them at a level not seen since Facebook started tracking me. Having researched No. 89, I learned this guy was born in captivity in Idaho in 2011. There are under 600 of these massive birds remaining in the world. To have the rare opportunity to see one was magical, but to be able to sit next to one for 30 minutes as I ate lunch was something spiritual, equivalent to petting the gray whales in Baja.

As I sat eating my lunch, the condor and I constantly exchanged gazes. Every so often, it would spread its wings to show off its true size. Not only did it not seem bothered by me, it seemed to enjoy my company (I mean, who doesn't?). After about 30 minutes, I began wrapping up lunch, and as I packed up, No. 89 silently turned away, spread its wings, and leapt off the rock like a hang glider sailing down about 100 feet and then turning upward, it flew off into the distance.

This magical encounter reinvigorated me for the 4.5 mile hike to the base of the mountain. I had a solid buzz from the encounter for the remainder of the day. Just like all the close encounters I have had in nature that buzz never seems to fade, and it has me looking forward to National Park Number 51.

Baja in the Slow Lane

For a motorcyclist, one of the easiest and most rewarding trips a rider can undertake is Baja, Mexico. It's a 1 day drive to the Mexican border from most of the Southwestern United States. I have been fortunate enough to spend many months in Baja over the past four years, but I always mixed the experience in with working, so I was never able to fully detach and enjoy it. For my fourth time riding Baja, this had to change. I wanted to allow myself to embrace this epic part of Mexico at a slower pace and savor each day. It's Baja. This is the time and place where you are meant to slow down and relax.

The week prior to my departure, a friend gifted me this giant stuffed sloth for my birthday. I promptly named him Slothykins. That name seemed to fit since I already traveled with a little stuffed lamb named Lambykins. Two days before departing for Baja, while packing my gear, I noticed the sloth in the corner of the equipment room staring aimlessly at the wall.

At that moment, an idea hit me. Now, usually (always) my ideas are a bit... off, and this one would prove no different. My thought was to use my Rok Straps to secure the giant sloth on the passenger seat of my BMW GS1200 and ride the 3,000-mile round trip from Sedona to Todos

Santos. What better way to embrace the slow lane of Baja life than with Slothykins as my passenger!

As I slowly departed Sedona, it wasn't long before I noticed something moving around in my rearview mirror. I quickly pulled over and saw everything was secure, and started again. I was in 3rd gear and again saw a flickering of movement. It turns out it was Slothykins. If I went above 50mph, his arm would begin flapping in the wind, and it gave the perception that he was waving at everyone. The whole scene was hilarious. Other vehicles along the road would slow down, scratch their heads or wave back to Slothykins as we happily motored along desert backroads on our way to Mexico.

One thing I didn't factor into this whole scheme was the attention I would receive once crossing the border into Mexico. This usually is a non-event; however, with Slothykins, I was promptly ushered into the "This guy definitely requires a further search" lane, to include an over friendly German Shepard. The dog performed a thorough job of sniffing Slothykins and the rest of my gear. It took a few minutes of the dog jumping all over the BMW before the Mexican Immigration Agents cleared me to proceed. Welcome to Mexico, Slothykins!

After the border dogs provide you with their approval to enter Mexico, your senses are instantly overwhelmed with the sights and smells of fresh food. At the same time, your mind awakens to the new obstacles in the road to include but not limited to horses, donkeys, cows, potholes, and large trucks along narrow roads with no shoulder. This sensory awakening can make you pretty hungry. Finding some street tacos and a strawberry Fanta from one of the many vendors you pass by is a rather easy task in Mexico. While sitting on the sidewalk, I begin enjoying one of the most delicious meals I've ever had. Meanwhile, I look over to see my motorcycle parked with Slothykins as a sentry keeping a watchful eye on the new surroundings. THIS is life at its finest in the slow lane of Baja, Mexico!

Baja is a thin peninsula with only four main highways, so when you meet fellow travelers along your journey, it is more than likely you will bump into them again at some point. The people of Baja have very kind hearts, so running into them repeatedly is a great way to build relationships along this journey. It didn't take long for me to inherit the nickname "The Sloth Guy." I found that name comical since I am a rather fast rider (ask any Massachusetts State Trooper).

For the next two weeks, with Slothykins as my tent mate and passenger, we happily camped on some of the world's most beautiful beaches while riding almost the entire length of Baja to a turnaround point on Playa Pescadero, which was just south of Todos Santos. I never tired of hearing "Hey Sloth Guy, come over for a beer" or "Sloth Guy wants to join us for dinner?" The hospitality is incredible in Baja, more so for motorcyclists, and as I learned, even more so for motorcyclists with a giant sloth as a passenger.

With the relaxing two weeks nearing an end, there was an outstanding question that I had to answer. What should become of Slothykins? I couldn't keep him as he was much too large, and I already had the immense responsibility of Lambykins, who is quite the handful. An idea hit me on the final night in Kiki's Camp in San Felipe. Why not donate Slothykins to an orphanage? After some time on Google and Google Translate, I happened to find the manager of a local orphanage called Sonshine Hacienda, who lived just a few blocks from where I was camping. I called him, and he was an expat who had been living in Baja, managing the orphanage for several years. I promptly drove over, met him, and donated Slothykins to his new home to where he would become a big hit and make many new friends. On the return ride to Arizona, the bike felt a bit lighter without my buddy on the back, waving happily at passersby. While crossing back into the United States, I smiled at the border agent while reflecting on the ride, the people, and the beautiful experiences over the past two weeks of traveling through Baja, Mexico.

A Whale of a (Baja) Tale

As someone who is always seeking adventure, I may have gotten in over my head with this one. I was three years in living full-time off my motorcycle, currently in Baja, Mexico, and navigating through a global pandemic. Not enough? Let's throw in a rescue mission at sea to ensure I have everything covered. Sure, why not?

It was a dark and stormy night, and the sea was angry...actually, it was just a bit windy around midday when I decided to partake in a whale watching trip on pangas. Pangas are small wooden boats in Guerrero Negro, Baja, Mexico. It's a magical encounter with nature as these majestic whales. These animals are the size of a school bus and will swim up to your panga. Once they do you can actually pet and cohabitate with them on a very personal level. It is a magical and life-altering experience.

Our tour begins with a standard safety briefing, and then we are bused out to the docks and fitted with life vests. Everyone is excited to get out and see these beautiful animals up close. Before boarding our panga, I noticed another boat with eight senior citizens leaving at the same time as mine and for a minute thought maybe I should jump in their boat as there were fewer people than on my boat, but I chose to stay where I was assigned with 12 people aboard.

The tour was going smoothly, but not great, as there was a lot of chop in the bay, so the whales didn't get as close as we'd like since the boat was bumping up and down. As the tour seemed to be ending, I noticed we began heading away from shore, but in a direction we hadn't been. At first, I thought they had spotted more whales as we all saw a giant gray object in the distance bobbing in the water. Once we got a bit closer, I realized it was not a whale at all but a capsized panga with three people clinging to the upside-down vessel by the propeller. The reality set in as we all took in more of the scene and began to see others floating in the water along with backpacks, camera bags, and purses. I quickly placed everything I had into a waterproof compartment in my rain jacket and handed it to another person on my vessel. I realized it was the panga with the eight seniors and said, "I guess I am going for a swim."

As we moved in to begin rescuing people from the water, I performed a headcount of those in the water. Knowing it was the panga with the seniors, I had all nine in my sight (eight and the captain), accounted for and saw they all looked to be relatively well. Although it was windy, it wasn't too cold. I also remembered from the safety briefing that there were no sharks in this part of the bay. I quickly realized no one was in immediate danger.

This is where it gets fun, sort of. As with all "disasters", there's "that guy." The guy who has to be a hero, no matter how little they know. We were "fortunate" enough to have one on our panga (dammit). The captain of our boat spoke little English but was very competent and was trying to give directions that seemed to be drowned out by the time they reached everyone. This was because our newly unelected hero was shouting his own orders on how to handle the situation. Our hero clearly knew best (he didn't).

Knowing the people in the water were not in immediate danger, I sat back on the far side of the boat as a ballast (Baja tacos assist in helping one become a great counterweight), shook my head, and let the hero begin to rescue people. He began clumsily and haphazardly pulling people out of the water and into our vessel incorrectly. While this was going on, I kept contemplating the consequences of throwing him overboard and rescuing the remaining seniors myself. Would saving eight people but leaving one to swim back result in any criminal charges against me in Mexico? Luckily for him, that was a fleeting thought.

One haunting moment that really still stands out is when the captain had to re-angle the panga to rescue the last three people clinging to the propeller. Those people remaining in the water thought we were leaving them and began shouting, "Don't leave us, please don't leave us." You could hear the fear and panic in their voices. Once we were angled properly, our "hero" had realized his uselessness and backed off, allowing us to properly load the remaining three people safely into the panga without issue.

The boat trip back to the docks was a quiet and bumpy ride. Everyone was soaked, including me (and I never even left the boat). There were three ambulances at the docks by the time we reached them. It was wonderful that no one required them other than for warm blankets.

Feeling great back on dry land (not as great as the nine that were in the water), I returned to the tour office. I met the owner of the tour company and began explaining the adventure in great detail over tequila and tacos. He brought out his guitar and played requests for us for several hours. I was planning on leaving Gurreo Negro that afternoon, but after the adventure, the tacos, and especially the tequila, I chose to stay one more night. After all, it's Baja, what's the rush?

Let my Turtles Go!

As you travel through Baja Mexico and encounter so many beautiful and unique experiences that you won't find anywhere else in the world, you really begin to appreciate all this area has to offer. This beauty arrives in the form of not only the people and their culture, but also in the form of raw nature that thrives on this magical peninsula. This rugged and hostile environment at first glance may not seem that inspiring, but once you look closer and begin to absorb your surroundings, you quickly realize how fragile, yet adaptable, this ecosystem is.

This is true of plant and animal life surviving in the driest of deserts on the peninsula. It also holds to the sea life along the rugged Pacific Coast, having to overcome predators and violent ocean conditions. It seems the challenges for life to overcome never cease here. The encounter I am about to share with you highlights these conditions as well as the resiliency of nature to survive here.

Every day from around the 1st of December through the end of February, there is a small, greenhouse looking hut along the beach just north of Todos Santos. The waves from the Pacific Ocean crash with such a concussion you almost feel nauseous from the vibration. This remote beach is where you can experience a magical wonder of life, baby sea turtles crawling into this violent ecosystem as their first test in their new world.

The baby sea turtles hatch in the early evening, and groups of four or five are placed into several plastic buckets by volunteers to await their release into their new world just after sunset. Timing is critical here because if they are released any earlier in the day, predatory birds are still out and will likely swoop in to gobble them up.

Once the sun begins to set, it is time to set these little creatures free. We each take a bucket and walk about 20 feet away from where the surf is crashing and tip the bucket, thus releasing the sea turtles to crawl out onto the still sun-warmed sands.

Once these little guys exit the bucket, it is difficult to imagine what they are thinking as they scurry towards the water with waves between 6-12 feet pummeling towards them. Some are fortunate and will hit the tide correctly, and the water will suck them out to the safety of the ocean. Others will miss the tide and will be tossed back violently 10-20 feet where they will start over. When this happens, you can hear a collective "Awwwww nooooo!!" from the group of us releasing them.

Ultimately (after three or four tries for some), all the baby sea turtles make it into the mighty Pacific Ocean just as the sun is fully dipping below the horizon. This is a beautiful piece of Baja life that should not be missed. I am very thankful to the Todos Tortugueos Volunteer organization for making this nightly event possible for the public. It is truly a Baja experience not to be missed.

The Legendary Fung Wah Bus

Throughout my life, I have tended to do a LOT of dumb stuff. Almost daily, everyone around me is questioning how I am still alive. This is no exaggeration, but there is one activity I partook in that is by far the most reckless. That is riding on the Fung Wah Bus. Recently, I was in a bar in Boston (yes, imagine that), and I was telling the story of the Fung Wah bus, which entertained the entire bar for close to an hour. My stories of this legendary form of transit must have been quite epic, as when cashing out, I was told my entire tab had been paid. So I thought a write-up on my experiences around this hazardous mode of transportation would make for a fun read.

The Fung Wah Bus isn't in service anymore for reasons described below. It was a $10 bus ride from South Station in Boston to Chinatown in New York City. I was 27 years old, living just north of Boston. A close friend was in New York City. The bus always arrived on time, there was no hassle with airports, and it was just easy.

I was alerted to the dangers of this bus when I arrived at work on Monday. My manager asked what I had done that weekend. I replied that I had gone to Manhattan to hang out with a friend. He asked how the flight was. "Flight?" I asked. "I didn't fly. I took the Fung Wah Bus." He doubled over laughing and said he paid me enough to do better. His comments were followed by several explicit adjectives. I still heard him ranting about it an hour or so later. I was a bit taken aback.

It didn't take long for me to realize the history of this bus and the numerous safety violations and failed inspections that made taking this bus not only risky, but in hindsight, downright dangerous. Massachusetts had even shut the service down a few times over the years. These buses were flipping over, catching on fire, and wheels were falling off. Outside that, though, the buses ran on time, no matter the amount of traffic or weather conditions. They had this trip down to an art. It was so honed that once, when I was stuck in traffic on the Cross Bronx Expressway, a few cars in front of me, I spotted a Fung Wah bus. Here's my chance! I followed it off the expressway as it zigged and zagged through the narrow surface streets until it returned to the now less-congested expressway. I felt like a running back following a lineman as a blocker until I could see the end zone. What a rush!

With it being a 4-hour ride, the driver would always stop at a Roy Rogers Restaurant for a few minutes to allow you to stretch, grab a bite to eat, and pray to the God of your choice for a safe remainder of the trip. To this day, having driven that stretch hundreds of times in my car, I have never seen that restaurant unless I was on the Fung Wah. Wherever the bus exited the highway, we all went into Narnia.

At the end of the day, the Fung Wah never disappointed, and although the bus was decommissioned like Old Ironsides, it provided some great stories and an economical way to get to New York City. As I sat in a Boston bar finishing my Sam Adams, I was thankful to the mysterious patron who got my tab. I am fortunate that this experience (riding the Legendary Fung Wah Bus) crossed my path.

Cuba Bound

I had just finished a certification exam that required more studying than I care to discuss. It was December 2008, and I was mentally exhausted and in much need of a beach vacation to reward myself for passing this rigorous exam. At the time, I happened to be visiting Montreal and decided to hit up a travel agent to see what deals were available. My only criteria was sun, beach, and relaxation. It is rare that I ever take time to slow down, even on vacation. It seems most of my vacations leave me more exhausted than relaxed (even though they are pretty rewarding). At this juncture in my life, I needed a "time out" to bask in the accomplishment of passing that exam, so I wasn't looking for anything too adventurous.

The travel agent in Montreal listened to my criteria and recommended Mexico or Cuba. As a citizen of the United States I was not allowed in Cuba. I asked the agent, she assured me it was not a problem. Cuba was much less expensive than Mexico, it would meet my beach requirements, and it was off the beaten path since Americans were not formally supposed to travel there. Cuba it is!

The flight to Havana was a short 3 hours from Montreal, and I was already yearning for a Cuban cigar and a glass of Havana rum while admiring sights along the white sand beaches. Once the flight began to descend, it hit me as I could see the last of the Florida Keys fading away from the plane window, "Wow, I wonder how much that travel agent really knew about the embargo for Americans." I was about to find out.

Feeling a little bit nervous as I entered the immigration queue, I saw those ahead of me enter this little glass box. The doors closed, they showed their travel documents, and once the doors opened on the other side, they were officially in Cuba. At my turn, I entered the glass box, it closed, and I showed my American passport for the immigration agent to view. He said "Uno momento" and went back to gather with four other agents who looked at me, then at my passport, and began passing it around like a Mickey Mantle rookie card. Ahhhh, this is how my Locked Up Abroad episode would begin, I thought.

The Cuban people love Americans, and it is so rare an occurrence to see an actual American passport that it draws a lot of curiosity. Something that I wasn't particularly looking for. When the agent went to stamp my passport, I quickly remembered about the embargo. A Cuban stamp in my passport would not go over well when I returned to the United States next week.

"No Stamp por favor", I said nervously. He laughed, said "No problem" and opened the glass box for me to enter Cuba. I made it! This is so cool!

What little I knew of Cuba was that my entire wallet was now useless. Health insurance, credit cards, and ATM access: Nothing would be accepted in this country due to the embargo. I had about $200 Canadian and reservations to an all-inclusive resort to ensure I could enjoy a week relaxing and not worrying about the limitations due to a lack of cash. This idea worked perfectly, with the exception that my travels would be limited to short day trips near the resort in Veracruz, and it wouldn't allow me to visit Havana.

This was all fine with me. I was able to relax at the beach while still having the ability to leave the resort to take in some local food and sights.

This included cigar stores, drooling over the 1950s cars that were still in pristine condition, and of course soaking up some much-needed sun. The resort where I was staying was filled with Canadians, and whenever they had those silly contests in the evening, they would always ask where the person was from. I was tempted every time I was called upon to grab the microphone and loudly say "The United States of America," and then I would revel in the silence that was sure to follow that statement. For once, I listened to my Dad's advice (Don't do anything stupid, Mike). For the entire trip, I identified as a Canadian from Toronto (I couldn't say Montreal as I didn't speak French), and I successfully avoided the temptation to say otherwise.

As the week came to a close, I had a great tan. I was relaxed and refreshed both mentally and physically. Mission accomplished!

Once we began our descent into Montreal, a revelation hit me: I still had to re-enter the United States, with a tan, in January, from Montreal. Would the US Immigration agent know I was in Cuba?

When the plane hit the tarmac, I did what any mature person who thought they were about to get into trouble does. I phoned my Mom and let her know that I may have overstepped, and she may be receiving a call from the US State Department in reference to my traveling shenanigans. After hanging up the phone, I felt a tap on my shoulder. It was a friend I had made at the resort. He happened to be sitting behind me and overheard the conversation with my Mom. He let me know that I could use him as an alibi and that he was a member of a health club in Montreal that had tanning beds. That seemed to be a solid response to any questioning I might soon face. I'll go with that, I decided.

I began to feel a bit more confident as I nervously drove into Vermont. The US Immigration officer had no questions for me and said, "Welcome home, Mr. Huber," as he waved my car onward. It was only about 10 degrees that night, yet I still could feel the warmth from the Cuban sun glowing. While breathing a sigh of relief, I happily drove by the "Welcome to the United States of America" sign. Cuba let me accomplish all my relaxation goals and tacked on a pretty cool story along the way.

Outriding the Pandemic

It was April, and it was warm, even for the Arizona desert. A steady easterly breeze made the heat of the mid-day sun tolerable. I roared down back roads of the high plains that curved in wide arcs, past abandoned tourist traps and teepee hotels from the golden age of auto travel. The boxer engine of my BMW GS were humming, interrupted by the whisper of dust devils that would whirl in from nowhere and dance in the center line like mini tornadoes. I twisted the worn black rubber grip of the throttle and let myself slip into a deep state of attention to what the moment required. I was fully bonded with the machine that hurled me northward toward an ice cold India Pale Ale and a desert campsite I had yet to meet.

It had been some time since I felt this content and at peace. Over the past three months, I had been watching the world burn down around me. My pandemic hideout in Mexico felt like a grandstand seat at the races, and I had been awaiting a fiery crash at the finish line. I soaked in the sun's rays through my riding suit and rolled the throttle on, savoring the feeling of heading home after months of uncertainty. Although riding north that day on Highway 89 was a fleeting moment, it clicked and whirred in my memory like a Polaroid snapshot of harmony and integration with my surroundings. I liked the feel of the TKC70 tires gripping the hot asphalt as I leaned the heavy machine through the corners with precision. It was the first time these tires had gripped American blacktop in 10 weeks. I could almost still smell the breeze coming off the Sea of Cortez mixed with a slight hint of burning garbage like you get in Mexico, along with the promise of wild nights, like it was before the plague sent us all running for the shadows.

Five Weeks Earlier

I woke up in a turquoise room. The sun's rays filtered in through translucent white curtains, embroidered with the flowers and skulls of Mexico's Day of the Dead. Loreto is a colonial beach town on the inland side of the Baja Peninsula. The room, an Airbnb, was my home this week. I woke up slowly from an abnormally deep sleep. I blinked several times and let the humming of the air conditioner and the slow building sound of traffic on the street outside remind me where I was. I felt the stiffness of a slight hangover in my body. I caught a flash of last night's events: Augie's bar. A roar of laughter, music, and conversation. I remember going into it looking forward to the fresh lime and rock salt taste of Margaritas and catching up with a couple riding GS800s. We had been playing leapfrog for several days as we all made our way down and then up the peninsula.

I don't know if you know any soldiers, or infantry soldiers, or paratroopers, for that matter, but we have a way of taking things to excess. There are a lot of reasons for it. Human behavior experts will cite the scientifically low levels of impulse control found in those who perform dangerous jobs. Some blame the adrenaline. Some say it's testosterone (women have it too, so don't even start). Whatever it is, I think it has something to do with getting whatever enjoyment you can from life, while you can. The couple with the GS800s had some spectacular stories of their travels. I was not one to pass up an opportunity to swap tales of two-wheeled adventure or pass up the highly flammable margaritas at Augie's.

I got out of bed quietly and filled the small, hotel style coffee maker with bottled water and some ground coffee that was dark and smelled promising. I liked the room. Sunlight streamed in and reflected off the brightly colored tile floor. A pair of parakeets outside the door were saying "buenos dias" over and over again to me, or maybe to each other. Either way, it sounded extra loud. I blamed the cocktails from the night before as I took that first magic sip of black coffee. I eased myself into a faux leather love seat and cracked open my laptop. I logged onto the VPN and started preparing to get some work done when the Google News hit me like the concussion from a grenade. The US State Department had raised its global travel advisory to Level Four, something that had never happened before. Not ever. The message left no room for interpretation: "Return home now or plan to hunker down wherever you are for an indefinite period of time." This was DEFON 4, for real.

As those words sank in, my phone began to chirp with messages from friends and family north of the border. They were relaying the CDC and State Department warnings, and trying to figure out where I was, and pushing for my hasty return. The World was officially in a biological crisis, something we had prepared for during my time in the 82nd Airborne but had always prayed would never really happen. A few moments later, my boss messaged me about COVID-19 and wanted to know if I was safe and sheltering in place. I told her that I was in Mexico and wasn't exactly sure what to do. She corrected me and said, "You mean you are in New Mexico?" I told her no. I am in old Mexico, like the real Mexico, on the Baja Peninsula, looking out over the Sea of Cortez at that very moment. There really wasn't much to say after that, and I was left alone with my phone, which went back to chirping along with the parakeets. I took another sip of coffee. I had some decisions to make. Although living free has some incredible benefits, like, well... freedom, lightness of being and of course the eternal spontaneity. Always the lurking fact that having too many options can create a kind of analysis paralysis. As a wise man once said, "Many a false move was made by standing still." For those of us who suffer from a lack of impulse control, standing still is not really an option. So I threw on my trusty Levis and prepared for action.

I stepped out into the street and realized that an eerie silence had settled in over the town. I had passed through this way about four weeks ago. At that time, it had all the trappings of a Baja tourist town; the bustling bars, restaurants, crowded sidewalks, coffee shops and art galleries. The historic Spanish Mission settlement of Loreto was now a ghost town. The streets were empty. Most of the businesses had closed, and many displayed signs warning tourists to return to wherever they came from. Within a couple of hours, the decision had been made. It was time to ride north.

I loaded up the BMW and headed out on Highway 1 North towards Gringolandia. Highway 1 is one of the most beautiful roads I have ever been lucky enough to ride. You navigate perfectly paved mountain switchbacks, complete with barrel cactus and rattlesnakes sunning themselves on the road. Then you begin a gradual decline towards the sparkling aquamarine blue water of the Bay of Conception. I decided to camp at a pristine little cove called Playa Santispac, a few miles south of the little mission town of Mulege.

I set up camp in a beachfront palapa and had just set about gathering firewood when a couple in an RV next door waved me over to join their fire. I could smell mouth-watering carne asada, seasoned to perfection, sizzling over the flames. I dropped the firewood and said I'd be right over. As I moved into the firelight, I noticed another couple was already sunk comfortably into camp chairs at the fire, cold Coronas in hand. It took all of a second to realize I met this couple a month prior. I been navigating the dirt roads way down on the southern tip of Baja outside of Cabo Pulmo National Park. I passed a couple of hours with these folks then, swapping stories and trading experiences and recommendations from the road. The world had still been a carefree and dreamy place a month ago. For a second I slipped into thinking about how quickly things had changed. Now, enjoying a fire and a seaside campsite together, we picked up right where we left off, telling stories of where we'd been and where we were going from here. North. The best thing about that evening was that no one mentioned COVID-19, or the world beyond the glow of that campfire, or the anxiety that was steadily growing inside me.

We ate carne asada tacos right out of the cast-iron pan and clinked shot glasses of tequila to the sound of small waves lapping the shore. I watched the last light of the sun disappear behind silhouetted palms and scattered palapas to the west. I thought that Baja must be one of the world's most beautiful places. It felt solitary and secure. It felt like it was ours. Without anyone saying it, we knew we were existing in a sort of bubble of denial. We were living in a nostalgia for the carefree times, which have now given way to something else, something less innocent to say the least. Denial and tequila are a pretty good recipe for happiness, at least for a while, and we all enjoyed the warmth of each other's company and the peace that the campfire afforded us, even if it was just for one night.

Threading the Needle

Definition: Safely navigating a path through significant or numerous obstacles, which may be either social, figurative or physical in nature. In base-jumping, threading the needle refers to passing through a narrow gap between terrain features, probably while wearing a wingsuit or squirrel suit, which generates lift and allows a controlled descent that feels like flying. Wingsuit flights usually end in the deployment of a parachute, or in death.

If you follow my road journal, you will know that I have been living off my motorcycle for the past three years. One thing I have learned in that time and those miles is the value of building solid friendships with the many amazing people I have met. One of these people is the Airbnb host I stayed with back in February when our Baja adventure was beginning. Veronica reminded me of Blanche from The Golden Girls. She was a blonde American woman from California. She had a high style and a kind of radiant energy about her. There were numerous stories of lovers past and present, and affairs won and lost like battles to a soldier who has traveled the world. Veronica recently retired from a nursing career, and she administered her Airbnb with a level of caring and perfection fitting to that career. Veronica had adapted quite readily to the slower paced life of the Baja in the safe little community of San Felipe. She was one of the warmest people I had met on this trip and made a point to keep in contact with her over the next two months as I explored every inch of the peninsula on my bike. When the pandemic started ramping up, she sent me a text message to check on me and, learning that I was still in Mexico, again offered to shelter me at her home.

San Felipe was just a 2-hour ride to the border. This appeared to be an option I did not want to turn my back on if I were to come down with COVID. Additionally, it seemed like I could remain pretty isolated in Baja. It was a peninsula; not counting the countless maritime options, there was really only one way on and one way off that thin little strip of sand. Even if you counted boats, access to Baja was a lot more controlled than, say, Mexico City, and my beloved USA was starting to look like a full on dumpster fire if the TV and internet news sources could be believed. Plus, from what I could see, the residents of Baja seemed to be more or less following the health protocols of the CDC and the World Health Organization. I planned to thread the needle and return to America once the cases leveled out there or began to decrease.

Essentially, I planned to cross the border after the worst had passed in the US but prior to the virus wave hitting Baja, which I knew it eventually would. I feared that if I stayed too long in Baja, sooner or later, as gringos, we would be seen as part of the problem, and I would become persona non grata.

The delayed evacuation plan was based on zero scientific data, but seeing the massive amounts of misinformation already circulating on the ever trusting internet, a gut feeling was the only impulse I could trust. One thing was certain: I had to set up a secure forward operating base. Veronica's house was located about three miles from the beach. It was the perfect place to wait and see what direction the world would go. This was an ideal launching point to counter most, if not all, scenarios I came up with during an official risk assessment and brainstorming session conducted over a bucket full of ice cold mini Coronas.

For the next three weeks, I fell into a kind of routine: sleep late, eat a leisurely breakfast while consuming worrisome world news and catching up on emails, ride to the beach. Routine can be a soothing thing when facing the end of the world as we know it in a country that is not your own, whose government could turn hostile on you at the drop of a sombrero. As I hovered over my laptop screen in the terracotta-and-pastel-stucco tactical operations center, I thought of the thousands of Mexicans who make the daring run across the border every day and the hostility they have to face at every stage of the journey

The big question was if and when to leave San Felipe and head for the border crossing at Calexico. There was no good advice, and there were no right answers. The world had not seen a pandemic of this magnitude in a hundred-plus years. There was certainly no guidance for people in my unique situation, living off the meager possessions that could fit on the back of my trusty GS motorcycle, far from home and making blind decisions that would affect (and possibly drastically shorten) my life. During this period of limbo in San Felipe, I was continuously urged by family and friends to return home to America. These pleas were nonstop and utilized a progressive escalation of force and coercion. I was grateful for the concern of everyone, especially my

Mother, who has patiently put up with more stupid and risky adventures than any mother deserves to. I made my entry to adult life as a paratrooper and moved on from the Army to world travel to my present decision to live as a motorcycle vagabond. Although I am not much for looking in the rear-view, I regretted momentarily all I put my Mother through every time I heard the worry in her voice over the phone, or sensed it between the lines of one of her text messages.

I received automatic updates from the State Department via email. These communiques were mostly just warnings to get the hell out of Dodge and come back stateside. I couldn't help but think, "Come back to what?" Since there was no cure and the numbers were steadily rising, it made no sense to return. I looked at the numbers, the collapse of health services and the mounting uncertainty and unrest in our country. In light of all that, every risk analysis I did, whether fueled by tequila, beer or black coffee, all pointed to battening down the hatches and weathering the storm at Veronica's Airbnb.

Once I decided to stay in San Felipe, I started to notice there was plenty going on in the community around me to cast some serious, escalating doubts on the very decision I had just made. The city was in a process of closing down and withdrawing from public life, just like I had seen in Loreto. Beaches and public entertainment venues were fully closed, and stores were boarding up one by one, making it more and more difficult to purchase food, booze and charcoal, all of which are non-negotiables. I ensured the BMW's gas tank was always topped off and kept the gear semi-packed. I was ready to go kickstand up within 15 minutes of any breaking news that provided a good enough reason to head north. The days started to blend together as I guess they did for a lot of people. I started to realize this was not going to be just another mini-crisis that passes and soon forgotten. The realization dawned on me that this was going to be a massive chapter in history, not only for North America, but for the world.

Through all the progressive shutting down of San Felipe, Baja and probably all of Mexico, one nearby beach remained open: Pete's Camp. This was a 3-mile ride from my Airbnb base, and it was a priceless afternoon getaway where I could relax on miles of empty beach that faced the beautiful blue waters of the Sea of Cortez. At Pete's Camp, my mind would drift, sometimes to the highest heights, memories of walking out the door of a C-130 into clear blue Carolina skies. Other times, it got dark on me, and I imagined a post-apocalyptic, post-COVID world. I didn't know which way the world was going to go. I didn't know if fear was going to dictate the next chapter in history or if courage and cooler heads would prevail. Occasionally, there would be a lonely RV parked at the camp, making its way north. Some were Canadians who still had a long road ahead. I would chat with these refugee travelers and worried retirees while awkwardly keeping my distance and trying to scavenge any credible news or credible rumors to supplement the politically partisan blame fest that we abused ourselves with daily online.

During a chat with a friendly couple of snowbirds from British Columbia, I learned that the Mexican Federales were refusing to let travelers go south. This rule made sense for Mexico since, at that time, COVID-19 was still more of a problem in the US. Unfortunately for me, I had to ride south a little way to get on the highway and head north. Heading due north from San Felipe led to nothing but open desert followed by a brick wall, or some wall, known as the US border. So, according to my land navigation skills, if I rode twenty miles east or west, I would risk being turned around on general suspicion of wanting to head south. If I made it to the highway, I could turn north. Still, if I failed to cross the border due to some Homeland Security snafu or some other unforeseen issue, I would likely not be allowed to return to San Felipe and my base at Veronica's because it would be, well… to the south. This scenario was not pleasant to think of. I imagined myself being forced into a fenced in refugee camp within sight of California soil, motorcycle confiscated, sitting cross-legged on the ground, and drinking rust colored water from cut off Tecate cans. With that vision in my head, I suddenly started feeling some empathy for all the countless people who had been in this position every day for decades, trying to head north, with Mexico saying 'go on, then' and the US saying 'whoa, not so fast' and a hell of a lot less resources in their pockets than I had at that moment.

Boxed In

I was boxed in, for my own safety, also for the safety of everyone around me. I thought about how many times public safety had been used as the reason to keep people from doing what they wanted, whenever the heck they wanted to do it. This pretty much described my life since I left the military, and especially these last three years living off a motorcycle. Under normal conditions, being stuck in a situation like this would cause a significant amount of stress, and it did, but under the new COVID-19 circumstances, it provided me with peace of mind, too. The fact was, there were about a thousand percent fewer people traveling the highways and byways of northern Mexico these days, and under the current circumstances, fewer people was good.

Although I knew how fortunate I was to be weathering this terrifying time in such a beautiful place, the harsh reality began to seep into my life. My work assignments were starting to dwindle. The thought of being laid off in the face of a full on economic depression started to creep into my idyllic little Garden of Eden in the desert of northern Baja. After three weeks of sheltering in place at Veronica's house in San Felipe, the mounting stress of inaction became more painful than confronting my worst case scenario. I decided to head for Northern Arizona, about five hundred miles from my current location. Judging from the news, it seemed, at least the first wave of this pandemic that the incidence of new cases was stabilizing and even lowering in some places.

Green Light

Although I reviewed new options every day, sometimes every hour, I committed to Wednesday to be my weekly decision point day. That would allow me a comfortable two days to pack, and I would leave on Friday and make it to Northern Arizona by Sunday at the latest. When Wednesday finally arrived, when I made that critical decision, my confidence wasn't high, but it was moderate, and I could work with moderate. Friday rolled around, and I psyched myself up and told myself that it was finally time to leave. I said goodbye to Veronica, assuring her that once I was safe in America, she was welcome to come and stay if the virus hit Baja as badly as I thought it would. I once again loaded the panniers covered with stickers from all the states I had visited. I leaned hard to the right against the added weight and let the kickstand flip up into place. I took a slight detour down the dusty dirt road I had ridden so many times to say a 60mph goodbye to the beach at Pete's Camp. I was finally returning home to the United States of America.

New World

Contrary to my apocalyptic daydreams, I crossed the border without incident. I waited in an almost non-existent line that consisted of a few cars, pickups and RVs, and pretty soon I handed my passport to a friendly Customs and Border Protection officer wearing a surgical mask. He accepted my documents and gave them a once over, not too fast and not too slow. "Welcome home." He said. I twisted the throttle and I picked up some of that quiet BMW speed, once again on good American asphalt.

It was still early and cool for Southern Arizona, so I stopped at the first beige stucco and Spanish tile Starbucks that came into view. I dismounted and shook off the vibrations, both real and metaphysical, as I walked up to a sterile window, where I was handed two cups of drip coffee by a young girl wearing a contamination suit and the kind of face shield I'd use to grind the slag off a frame weld. I sipped bitter coffee and looked at my new reality. I tried to stay focused on the beauty of my surroundings and the success of an easy border crossing back to my homeland. I had avoided the refugee camp scenario, and I was very thankful and glad to be back on US soil.

Now that I was back in the United States, where was I supposed to go, and how would I adapt to this scary new world order as a motorcycle nomad? It was a relief to be back in my home country, but to what avail? Everyone and everything was fully locked down. Almost nothing was open, and no one had worked for weeks or months in some cases. It was a stark contrast to the America I knew just ten short weeks ago. There would be no gatherings with friends and family at my favorite bistro to share stories of my adventures in Baja. There would be no popping over to my favorite local watering hole for a cold Four Peaks IPA while catching up on local gossip.

Although I had been living in the same isolation south of the border just yesterday, it felt different now being home, because now I owned the problem. My country had been enjoying record high prosperity when I left just a few months ago, and record low unemployment. Now, huge numbers of Americans were unable to work and didn't know how they would pay their bills, rent or mortgages. I tried to keep my mood upbeat as I set up a cozy little camp that afternoon in the Prescott National Forest. I could have ridden straight through, but I wanted to be alone that first night, inhaling the aroma of dry pine on the breeze as I sat around a small fire. I needed the strength and clarity that came from sleeping that first American night on the clean, coarse sand of the high Arizona desert.

A sobering reality set in the next morning as I rode from first light through the lonely desert, now more deserted than ever. The whine of my 1200cc boxer engine and the wind in my helmet were the only sounds on the surreal Arizona landscape. That morning as I blazed on with the rising sun to my right, it felt like the whole country was on a one-way road northbound. I truly hoped that road wouldn't become a dead end. I continued north, avoiding the freeway, until the soft afternoon light came from the west. I felt the temperature drop a few degrees as I roared over Mingus Mountain Pass in the Coconino National Forest. I leaned extra low and deep into every curve, wanting the bike and the tires to be there for me, to reassure me and support me in this time of uncertainty.

Motorcycle riding can provide perspective. It can make existential problems feel distant, forcing you to focus on the here and now. As I descended into the still air and the evening warmth of Arizona, the light of the setting sun shone on the rocks, giving them a warm kind of alpenglow I had never noticed before. I knew that here, in the warm, safe interior of America, I would be able to find a moment of solace to shake off the culture shock, gather my thoughts. Next would be to lay out options for putting one tire in front of the other and ask myself: "Where to next?"

The world was changing, radically and daily. I needed a plan that would allow for continued mobility. I found a lot of courage there in

Arizona. From that place of courage, I realized that the sun would indeed rise again. It would also rise over Veronica's little house, where I had waited out the uncertainty of the first wave, and it would also rise over any lonely Canadian RVs still parked at Pete's camp, facing the Sea of Cortez and the new normal. So would it rise over our lives tomorrow and over the lives of our people near and far. Since my days in the 82nd Airborne, failure has never been an option, and this was no time to start considering it. I broke out the bottle of Laphroaig, and I began unrolling the maps. The Southwest Operations Center was now established. I got down to the serious business of where to next, knowing I'd be kickstand up in no time.

Tongariro Crossing, Tongariro National Park, New Zealand

The Tongariro Crossing in New Zealand is touted as one of the world's best day hikes. This obviously meant it was a hike I had to tackle. The crossing is 19.4 kilometers (11.64 miles) across an active volcano, and it includes a LOT of stairs, both up and down. Having not been hiking in several months, this was the first time I was actually questioning my physical ability. I don't think it comes from age as much as hard landings from falling out of airplanes. Either way, it's the Number 1 hike on Earth, so it really needed to be checked off my list.

As with all mountains, the weather is constantly changing, and this mountain would prove no different. The previous day, the hikes were cancelled due to heavy winds. Upon waking up at 0400, it was a relief to learn that the shuttles would be running that day. My campsite was just outside the town of National Park and was right along the shuttle path for a 0545 pickup and a 30-minute drive to the trailhead.

The hike started with misty clouds, which added to the already stunning mountain scenery, and the winds, well, they were blowing hard. I had purposely loaded my day pack heavy with extra everything in the event I'd need it. That was smart. By day's end, I had used almost everything I brought. This was comforting since I thought I had over packed.

The first five kilometers weren't bad except for the brutal winds that were a constant battle. It got to the point that when the winds subsided, I'd almost fall due to leaning in so much. Once those five kilometers were wrapping up, there were several posted signs that said, "If you aren't feeling well, now is a great time to turn back; there is no shame in that." I used those signs as motivation to continue.

Once reaching the summit, it was obvious the crown jewel of the hike would not be shining as brightly as it had been in the photos. There were two bright neon emerald green lakes that, in the sun, just glowed; however, with the weather having turned so quickly, it was nothing more than a dull blue barely visible through the cloud bank. The winds were still howling from every direction. There was hardly even time to snap a few photos before I decided it was time to descend into the next crater for some shelter and to take a break and eat a snack. The only portion that remained was the never ending descent filled with many more steps.

Overall, it was a magnificent day with great views and conversation with fellow hikers from all over the world. My finish time, not that it matters, was just over 6 hours. This seemed admirable as the estimated time for most was between 6 and 8 hours. The remainder of the day was spent at my campsite, swimming in my own personal grotto behind my tent, talking with others who hiked it (or would in the morning), consuming ibuprofen, and feeling semi-accomplished now that this hike was completed.

Memorial Day

Not being in the United States for Memorial Day and seeing our flag lining every Main Street throughout our country is one of those times I miss being home. Having served as a soldier in the United States Army, I have endless respect for those who lost their lives in defense of this great nation. I am now learning how to respect it even more so on a global level.

This year, on April 25th, my travels allowed me to celebrate a Memorial Day for two of our allies, New Zealand and Australia. While on a guided tour through Fraser Island, a remote sand island off the northeastern coast of Australia, our tour was delayed an hour at the ship wreck of the TSS Meheno HMNZ Hospital Ship 1. The Meheno was a critical resource in WW I in retrieving the wounded from Anzac Cove in Gallipoli for both New Zealand and Australia. When I asked why the tour was delayed, the guide explained, "Today is Anzac Day," and went into the meaning of this holiday.

Anzac Day is a combination of Veterans' Day and Memorial Day for both Australia and New Zealand. Once I learned this, I left the tour group and made my way into the heart of the ceremony before it began. I knew I was with my people here at this ceremony. I am not quite sure how I knew, but I just knew. It didn't take me long to be welcomed by the Australian Army Veterans partaking in the ceremony. They eagerly invited me to stand with them front and center to pay respects to their fallen and veterans. As many people know, I only own two shirts: an 82nd Airborne Division shirt and a Boston University shirt. This day, I was lucky enough to have worn the 82nd shirt, and it didn't go unnoticed by the Australian Army veterans. As the ceremony concluded, one of the veterans pulled me aside, thanked me and handed me an Anzac Day pin. I don't travel with much, but that pin is now part of my sensitive items list.

I was beyond humbled to be standing there, shoulder to shoulder with our allies as they laid wreaths, gave speeches, and played both the Australian and New Zealand national anthems. On more than one occasion, I teared up, and for good reason. These servicemen and women easily could have been backing any of our 6's as Americans. The ceremony resonated deeply within me in realizing that Memorial Day is much more far reaching than just our shores in the United States.

In the following month, I went further with what I took away from that Anzac Day Ceremony by taking the time to visit the Australian War Memorial in Canberra. This museum was as moving as any of ours would be in the United States. They have etched in the walls the names of each of their fallen from every campaign they participated in.

This includes the Tomb of the Unknown Soldier for Australia and an eternal flame.

I will forever remember my Anzac Day experience. This day is for our American fallen, it is important to know that these ceremonies go on for all our allies across the world. Please remember the reason for this holiday over the weekend and take the time to pay respects to our heroes of this great Country. God bless America, and God bless our Allies.

Ayers Rock 1: Coober Pedy

At the time of this writing, I was sitting in my hotel room, which happens to be in an underground cave in the tiny opal mining town of Coober Pedy. Normally, this would sound crazy, but 50% of the residents in this town live underground, so it's perfectly normal to be living as someone on the desert planet of Tatooine would live. It is deep in the Australian Outback, hundreds of miles from nothing. How I even ended up in this town is something I am still piecing together, but alas, here I am typing this up as an Aboriginal drum beats from the distant hills and echoes into my cave dwelling.

Having just two days off since leaving New Zealand in early April 2024. There were multiple countries I toyed with visiting. Australia kept being highly recommended from other travelers, but I didn't really feel the calling for it. So I was hesitant when I booked a one-way ticket to Sydney and was expecting a short stay to check the box. Life it seemed had other plans for me as I am currently six weeks into this giant country with no end in sight.

When I say no end in sight, I literally mean no end in sight. Having motorcycled much of the Southwestern United States over the past 6 years, I think I have a pretty solid grasp on distances and expansiveness with large pockets of isolation and nothingness. I knew what large areas were and how to negotiate them, even on two wheels. I couldn't have been more ignorant of what expansiveness really is.

Expansiveness is driving 100+ miles and not seeing another car, and only a random oncoming truck towing three or four trailers that, when it passes you, throws your tiny rental off the road due to the wind gust. Expansiveness is slowing down to some unknown road hazard in front of you, only to realize it's an emu that decides to attack your car, so you must quickly swerve and speed up. Expansiveness is clicking search on both AM and FM radio stations, only to have it indefinitely spin without a station to be found for hours. Expansiveness is Australia.

Australia is my home for the time being, and I am trying everything possible to do more than scratch the surface of this foreign and incredibly large part of the world. With every type of climate you can imagine and wildlife that is other worldly, cute, dangerous, and some a combination of the three. This series will take you through my journey in Australia as I make my way towards Ayers Rock (Uluru) in the great Australian Outback.

Ayers Rock 2: The Great Ocean Road

I will start this story with the disclaimer that my lack of planning and just going with the flow of Australia allowed for this adventure to even happen. I originally thought that I would easily be able to circumvent (I think that's the right word) the Australian continent in a month. Not a big deal. Yeah, some long days, but doable. If you go back to Part I of this story, you will realize I got hit by a brick daily on that theory. Either way, I had a rental car for a month and would see what adventures I could experience using a list two close friends had provided as a high level blueprint.

After a couple of days exploring Sydney, it was time to pick up my rental car, hit the open road, and embrace what would come while in Australia.

One of the first locations where I was able to slow down and take some time to embrace my surroundings was the Great Ocean Road. Having ridden some pretty incredible roads throughout the planet, for me to say much about any road is a rarity. This is one that I was kicking myself for being in a rental car (and not on a motorcycle).

The Great Ocean Road begins just west of Melbourne and extends to Port Fairy. It is 146 miles long. The road is paradise for anyone who has ever ridden a motorcycle. The entire length skirts the coast of the Southern Ocean from cliffs high above. "Breathtaking" doesn't begin to touch how this feels, as every corner provides a new panoramic view of rock formations and ocean as bright green as you can imagine.

Occasionally, the road cuts inland through thick rainforest. There are plenty of short hikes with gushing waterfall views in these parts. If you look closely, you will likely find a koala bear lazily eating eucalyptus leaves in a tree high above. Wallabies dance around your car, curiously peering in to see if anything is worth a closer inspection for something to fill their bellies.

Another beautiful feature of this paved paradise is the lack of people along the way. Several campsites I visited had no one in them. I am certain it helped that it was offseason (that and my ability to find off the beaten path locations). It wasn't odd for me to have miles of beach to myself while enjoying a cold VB Bitter beer. I could stare along the endless coastline while listening to the waves crashing, with my surroundings devoid of any other creature (with the occasional exception of a kangaroo hopping by).

Upon driving along the Great Ocean Road, my mind was in the right place. I was filled with peace through the solitude I enjoyed from star filled nights. I felt as though my mental clarity was honed, and I was prepared for the next part of my journey (that being the vastness of the Outback of Australia). On many levels, this would prove to be more challenging than I had imagined as I continued the long journey to my destination of Uluru, Ayer's Rock.

Ayers Rock 3: Arrival

Ayers Rock was my destination. This is not an easy destination to reach, especially by car. It takes dedication, time, and patience. Many people fly to this location and use tourist busses to get around in the park, snap a few photos, and leave. Not me. It is cliché, but I feel the journey is more important than the destination. What you see, hear, and feel along the way allows you to appreciate the destination when you do finally reach it. This two week drive to Ayers Rock elevated that cliché phrase to a level I never thought possible.

My original plan was to circle the entire continent of Australia in a month. That was NOT happening, so Ayers Rock (Uluru) was a solid turnaround point. Mind you, to even complete this took me one month. The isolation was beyond what I had expected. I knew going into this, that isolation would be the greatest challenge. What I didn't grasp was how far I would be pushed mentally during this journey.

To add to the trip, one of my best friends and a fellow paratrooper had been diagnosed with cancer a few years back, and I knew his time was coming. Our texts and calls were becoming more and more infrequent. Fortunately, I am very close to his sister. When I don't hear from him within a week, I reach out to her to obtain a status update.

During one of the most desolate spots on earth, I received a text from her to inform me of his passing.

You don't understand isolation until you receive a text like that in spotty cell phone coverage. There was no way of replying or reaching out to console and provide support to his loved ones. This left a more than significant gap in my mind, with no way of processing it since I was in the middle of the Outback. There is no one to rely on for comfort or a crutch to get you by. There is nothing, just nothing. The only consolation I found was hours of alone time to think and process it while focusing on how fortunate I was to have such a close friend, all the while driving for hundreds of miles with, again...nothing. A few dead kangaroos on the side of the highway, with an occasional eagle or dingo chomping on them, was the only life I saw through this portion of the drive.

Upon arriving at Uluru, I set up camp. My camp only entailed pulling into a parking spot as I was car camping. A solid positive to car camping is that there is minimal to no preparation, setting up or pulling down camp. After cooking a quick meal in my "campsite", I thought I had enough in me to drive around Ayers Rock for sunset.

Upon entering the park and seeing Ayers for the first time, my eyes welled up. I am not sure if it was due to this area being such a spiritual place for the Aboriginals or that the drive to reach it was so emotional. It really doesn't matter. To finally lay eyes on this magnificent rock glowing in the golden hour of sunset was a moment that will resonate with me forever. I was fully present in the moment and felt a sense of calmness.

After a semi solid night's sleep in the car, it was time to do a 3-hour hike around the rock and really get to experience this monument of the ancients up close and personal. Since I had been car camping in some warm climates, I purchased some mesh window covers to allow the windows to remain down in the evening without having any bugs, flies, snakes, kangaroos, or dingos enter the vehicle while I was sleeping. This purchase turned out to be one of my better decisions along this drive. Flies plague Uluru—an unimaginable amount of them. Starting the hike early in the morning was key to avoiding them, and as the sun rose over this great rock, having the car mesh as a makeshift fly screen for myself on the hike was a lifesaver.

Traveling alone through Australia is an experience that forced me to look at life from a unique perspective that many will never understand or even imagine existed. The month was filled daily with two constants: Change and being challenged to adapt to the environment. By environments, I mean both from the outside world and from the world within me. Both were deeply felt throughout my long journey to Ayers Rock.

Cambodia

Cambodia is another country that wasn't on my radar, but having been obsessed with experiencing all 7 Wonders of the World. I really wanted to see Angkor Wat. I know, I know. It isn't on the list of 7 Wonders now, but that list seems to be ever-changing, and I didn't want to miss out in the event it was added again. That, and the other reason, is that I was about to overstay my visa limit in Thailand (running my visas out seems to be a new talent of mine).

Originally, I booked a flight to Phnom Penh as a forward journey requirement for Thailand entry. As the time got closer to my travel, I linked up with a driver in Cambodia who would take me around to see the many Temples. However, upon sending him my flight itinerary, he quickly replied, "Dude, you are flying into the other side of Cambodia; Angkor Wat is 360 kilometers from that city." After 8 months, this was really my first error of any consequence. There were two options: a 6-hour bus ride or spend $80 and book a new flight. I chose the latter to save time.

Upon arrival, and a minor hiccup going through immigration (I didn't bring $30 for a visa, so I had to "borrow" it from an immigration officer, who required a hefty "tip"). It was part of the game, and another lesson learned from my poor planning. I can't complain. Once through customs, I met my driver, Kong, outside the airport and we were off to my hotel in Siem Reap.

The first thing I noticed in Cambodia (besides the fact that they drive on the right side of the road…it has been 8 months since I have been in a country that drives on the right) was the heavy humidity. It was brutal, even though I was in high humidity places over the past three months. This was the next level, and there just was no reprieve, even in the early morning and evening. Along the drive, we discussed my objectives while in Cambodia with the main one to see Angkor Wat. With the heat and humidity being so oppressive, Kong recommended we start at 0430 the next morning in order to see sunrise at the Temple. This would provide for a magnificent way to begin the day and allow us to get a head start on the heat.

We arrived at Angkor Wat at around 0530 and walked through the darkness and over the moat that guards this UNESCO treasure. All the while, the mountainous sandstone silhouette was gaining in color and depth as our path led toward a meeting point between us and the rising sun. Even during the off season, there was quite a crowd at the reflection pool, at sunrise, to try to get that perfect photo of this stunning homage to Hinduism. It didn't take long for the heat to follow. This was our queue to seek out shade deep within the Temple to avoid more heat and growing crowds. We then began exploring the hidden Temple chambers of this Temple.

The depth and detail of the Temple were more than impressive. Even with the destruction from past wars and an occasional bullet hole in the sandstone, the overall structure hadn't lost its mystical feeling. The mysticism was unavoidable as we walked through the Temple's many chambers.

Of the many experiences along my journey, I think Angkor Wat is one of the best things worth seeing, touching, and experiencing. Whether included in the 7 Wonders of the World or not, it makes little difference in my appreciation of this stunning structure. Even as a massive tourist attraction, this Temple sets the criteria for what an ancient wonder should be. Experiencing it was well worth the trip to Cambodia.

The Working from "Home" Years

Becoming a Digital Nomad: Testing the Waters

In 2010, the company I worked for gave me my pink slip due to budgetary cuts. I was feeling distraught and lost because I had been working there for 8 years. Fortunately, I had a great director who helped by transferring me from a management position into a project manager slot that would be fully remote.

Remote positions at the time were called working from home. It didn't take long for me to ask myself a question: What if I didn't have a home? This was mostly bar talk amongst friends, and I didn't expect the crazy scenarios we discussed to ever become a reality. Well...it seems planting those seeds in my mind was all it took for them to nurture, and then to grow into 13 years of almost nonstop travel.

The first two years were mostly spent learning to excel in my new position as a project manager, along with clumsily discovering how to adjust my work/life balance in creative ways which involved motorcycling throughout New England in between work responsibilities.

Something I learned early is that there are McDonald's with Wi-Fi everywhere, and at the time, it was one of the better places to stop to respond to emails or for a conference call (this was a life before riding a BMW, so I didn't require Starbucks). I timed my rides to reach these locations 10 minutes before conference calls. This allowed me time to set up and prepare for them as needed.

The first day as a remote employee, I decided to knock out a ride from Boston to Route 17 in northern Vermont. Route 17 is also known as the "Little Tail of the Dragon." It was May, and I was literally working off my Ducati Monster M1100 as I tore up Vermont. Since it took so long to reach Route 17, it made sense to ride it twice to ensure the long ride was worth it and regain the curve back in my tires. It may have been one of the best days I have ever had working, and I figured this newfound freedom would provide many opportunities to fill in the gaps that I had been missing by going into a regular office daily.

Riding all the way to Vermont from Boston on your first day in a new position probably was a bit of overkill. I was missing calls and hadn't noticed my phone was constantly ringing in my pocket (an easy oversight, being so heavily focused on riding). I was in flight formation and setting the pace for a flock of mallards that happened to be flying down the White River. This road ran parallel to Route 100. Unbeknownst to me, the phone continued ringing as the Ducati's Termignoni exhaust roared through the Green Mountains while I leaned into corners that followed the river.

Shortly after parting ways with the mallards and crossing back into New Hampshire, I saw some lights behind me. It was a New Hampshire State Trooper. Dammit! I am sure I was speeding, but the question always is how fast. It was fast. As I began talking to the State Trooper to try to minimize the damage, I could now hear my cell phone ringing. I picked it up as the Trooper ran my information. It was my new manager, based in Virginia, calling to introduce herself and ask if I had noticed that I had missed a call I needed to be on. I stated I was just out getting a coffee (This excuse was 100% true; it's just that the coffee was 200 miles away). This was probably one of my more challenging multitask scenarios (i.e., signing a speeding ticket while on an introductory call with my manager). To this day, I feel I would have been able to get out of that ticket had I not been so distracted by work. Lesson 1 as a remote employee learned.

After that day, I knew I should take my work a bit more seriously and slow my pace. I continued to ride, but always ensured I attended every call (which I did over the next 13 years). My work ethic has always been strong, and I didn't want to compromise this position and what I could do with it by losing my focus. Continuing to merge my work responsibilities with riding was something that I honed to an art form.

Once I was comfortable performing my work one or two days a week off the motorcycle, I thought I would step the adventure up a notch: California. I had relatives in Oakland, and there was a Harley rental in San Francisco, a short transit ride away. It made sense to fly there for two weeks and work remotely in a new environment and time zone to see how I would perform.

The test run couldn't have gone smoother. I was on Pacific Time when my team was on Eastern Time. This ensured that by 1:00 p.m., all my tasks and calls were completed. Having earlier workdays provided much more time to explore San Francisco and the Bay Area. A couple of vacation days in the mix allowed time to rent a Harley in San Francisco and take a 3-day trip to Tahoe and Yosemite. Even though I was on vacation those days, I felt obliged to join work calls whenever possible to stay on top of my projects, while obtaining bonus points from management for doing so on my time off. I felt this made up for my missed meeting when I first started this position in New Hampshire.

The California trip had solidified my ability to work from anywhere. On the return flight to Boston, my thoughts focused on a far-fetched mindset: What if I don't have a home? It would take a few months of planning and a solid leap of faith. As with all leaps of faith, you never know where or how it will end, but I felt sure I could make this dream a reality. What I didn't realize was how far I would take this and the new experiences my decision would deliver. I turned my life into Ferris Bueller's Day Off on steroids over the next 13 years.

Life as a Digital Nomad: Exiting the Wheel

It was May 2012, Boston was becoming extremely boring, and the thought that it might be time to expand my horizons began to grow inside my head. Remaining as a "work from home" employee and having traveled throughout most of the United States with not so much as a hiccup in missing calls or people asking, "Hey, where are you working from today?" Most wouldn't expect any response outside "my living room" or "the kitchen table" since that is what everyone was doing, and to think an employee was winding up roads in New England on an Italian sport bike or hanging out in Haight Ashbury in a coffee shop while leading a project team call was unthinkable. Now, many will read this and think I wasn't working and just touring the country while attending a call here and there. While that perspective isn't totally wrong, it isn't fully accurate, either. My organization was giving me awards every quarter, including project manager of the year. While this was all happening, our company was constantly laying people off to the point where morale was extremely low.

Even with my newfound freedom, I felt myself being dragged into the depths of depression due to the constant threat of layoffs. It was time to take this working from home to the next level. That being the "what if I don't have a home" plan. It wasn't much of a plan, but more of an execution of an idea born over a few beers in a dark Boston bar two years earlier.

As with everything in life, the first step is the scariest, but also the most critical to set the wheels in motion. After thinking this over for a bit, the most effective way to ensure I followed through with my plan of setting myself free geographically was to rent out my Boston condo. This was easier than I expected, and I had it rented through a management company in under two weeks. June 1st, my new tenant would move in. This was it. I was going to not have a home for at least a year. A timeline was now drawn for me to sell everything I owned and find out where my new "home" would be.

Somehow, I knew that returning to Boston wasn't going to be in the cards. Having a massive fire sale seemed the best way to clear my life of material possessions that were now just clutter, and there was a lot of clutter to be cleared. With time being short, it was an emotionless task to sell, donate, and give away almost everything. Paying for a storage unit for an unknown amount of time seemed pointless.

Once everything I owned was condensed into a small box of keepsakes and my travel backpack, it was time to decide where to go. As I looked around the condo, I was left with the question that I probably should have started with before taking all these drastic actions. Where the Hell am I going to go? This is one of those "I may have screwed up" moments.

Originally, the semi sorta kinda plan was to drive around the United States and spend a month or so in each state and see what became of it. As I was looking at a map, figuring out a few first stops on my new journey, my phone rang. It was a 617 Boston number, and I instantly thought it was a spam call. This is one call I am glad I didn't push to voicemail. It was one of my relatives whom I had gifted a Magic Jack plug a year or so ago. He was calling to catch up and let me know he had just moved to a house in the jungles of Nicaragua and had internet service that was just as fast as in the USA. My jaw dropped, and I threw the map of the United States into the trash can that was already overflowing with trinkets and other items that I felt would never be needed again.

Feeling so lost in the United States (on many levels), a new environment would not only be healthy mentally for me but might propel my work motivation (which was currently nonexistent). Right about this time, most of my friends and family were sure I had lost my mind. Going to Nicaragua on a one-way flight for an undetermined amount of time seemed reckless and a sure way to lose my job (some even felt my life would be in jeopardy).

Having previously traveled much of Central America, I knew most of these concerns were unfounded or pulled from a news article where one person had a bad experience. The news never really covers the thousands who traveled to this part of the world and had nothing but wonderful things to say about the people, the culture, and the sights that many will never know. Having grown up in Maine (where, for many, the fear of even venturing to Boston), it was incomprehensible for them that I would move to Nicaragua.

As I arrived in Maine, I parked the Ducati in the garage, closed the door, and wondered when I would next see that beautiful machine. Little did I know that it would be a year and a half before I would hear the magical dry clutch clacking again. Later that day, I boarded a flight out of Logan Airport. With reality setting in, I stared out the window. I was really doing this. Nicaragua was going to be my new home.

Nicaragua

My flight that had left Boston landed safely in Managua, Nicaragua, and I was ready to begin my next adventure working remotely. To ensure a smooth transition to a new country, I took a week of vacation so I could test out the Wi-Fi, adjust to the new environment, and take some time to relax after the whirlwind of tasks that had been completed before leaving the United States. Getting off the wheel that many are trapped in isn't the easiest or least stressful thing to accomplish. As I would later learn, it is much easier to re-enter the wheel than it is to exit it. To clarify, when I say "wheel", I am referring to how most live their lives with an apartment, car, routines, etc. There is nothing wrong with living a life inside the wheel, and I am not one to judge, but for me, it just felt wrong living that way. I am not sure if it was too cookie-cutter or if I found it monotonous and unfulfilling. Either way, the wheel wouldn't be something I had to think about for the foreseeable future.

Upon arriving in the tiny jungle village of El Rosario (a 2-hour mountainous drive from the humidity, crowds, and heat of Managua), I gazed upon my new home with glee. It was a small 3-bedroom ranch on about 4 acres of land with every plant, vegetable, and fruit you could imagine. All this beauty was just steps away from my hammock on the front porch, where I could relax and gaze out into the lush jungle.

Once my week of vacation was wrapped up, I began my usual work routine, but a tad different from that in Boston. The morning entailed going outside to retrieve eggs from the chickens, coconuts, pineapples, starfruit, dragon fruit, and, of course, some hot chilies to add a kick to breakfast. This area of Nicaragua was very secluded, so it wasn't long before I realized how much time I was spending working and really beginning to get out of my funk I had been in a few weeks prior.

After my 2nd successful week in El Rosario, I felt this would be my home for the next few months and wanted to add some more character to it. Running was a big pastime of mine. This activity helped me meet the locals and build relationships within the community. One of the neighbors had an amazing property to include a monkey named Paco. Paco was not very friendly, and it seemed after you gave him a couple of beers, he got even less friendly. Nevertheless, this was one of my favorite stops along my run (mainly since the owner would give me a beer or two to rehydrate). After chatting with him, I noticed he owned a couple of beautiful Rottweilers, and they had recently given birth to six cute little puppies. That was it: I bought two of the little guys for $30 and brought them back to the ranch.

Now my life in Nicaragua felt complete. I now had two badass little puppies that would join me every morning when I went out to gather food for breakfast. They would also make a great addition to the security of the property. This was disappointing to the neighbors who had a hole in their fence. It didn't take long before they noticed their chickens began to go missing. It seems the chickens had a curiosity about what was on the other side of the fence. Death. Death was on the other side of that fence. As soon as they meandered into the yard, there would be a loud squawk followed by an explosion of feathers, and that is how my new

153

pups were fed. Of course, this only went on for a couple of weeks until the neighbor became highly motivated to repair the hole in his fence.

After two incredible months of living in Nicaragua, working by day and spending the evenings in the hammock with my dogs lying next to me as I drank Flor de Caña rum, I started to think it may be time to move to my next location. The biggest and possibly only issue I had with living there was the isolation. I was miles from any town, I didn't have a car, and I was living essentially on a 4-acre compound. The property was surrounded by 8-foot walls with concertina wire on top. Don't get me wrong. It was a safe area and I never felt in danger, but the risk of theft or a break-in was always there. After a week debating whether to move or not, I decided to pack it up and take a 26-hour local bus ride to Panama. Once again, boarding a vehicle to a new destination, I felt stress just as intense as when departing Boston. Would Panama work out as well as Nicaragua?

Panama

Having just left my new home in Nicaragua and boarding a local bus on a 26-hour ride to Panama had me almost second guessing my decision. The bus was packed, and the bathroom already looked like a scene out of Poltergeist. Now, all this I was able to tolerate, but what really got my goat was that they had TVs every few rows. You'd think, "OK, I'll watch a few movies to pass the time." Not on this bus. They had a Kirk Cameron movie (Fireproof) on repeat AND in Spanish. I had never seen this movie, and by the 2nd time it rolled on, I was ready to just set up camp inside the destroyed bathroom to get a reprieve from it.

I eventually fell asleep with the help of some Flor de Caña that I smuggled onto the bus. After what felt like forever, the bus came to a stop, and I noticed everyone was getting off. I was still half asleep when I was ushered off the bus. Still bleary-eyed, I looked at my watch. It was 4:00 a.m. I was at the border of Nicaragua and Costa Rica, and the border crossing didn't open until 7:00 a.m. I was beginning to understand why the bus ride would take 26 hours. After sitting on the concrete for 3 hours, the border finally opened, and I was welcomed into Costa Rica.

Once back on the bus, my anxiety increased as I wondered what type of obstacles I'd have to overcome to enter Panama. Entering through the Panama border was less time-consuming. Still, again, the bus emptied and everyone was guided into a small room with their luggage, where everyone had to open each luggage item as dogs systematically sniffed through all the luggage, piece by piece. Then, once back on the bus, I continued the journey to Panama City. Fireproof was probably on its 8th showing.

The further south I traveled, the landscape continued to change, as did the neighborhoods. In Nicaragua, the houses were mostly in poor condition, but by the time I was in Panama, they were more like those you'd find in the United States, modern and well maintained. This was due to the Panama Canal, which draws in an unreal amount of revenue for the country.

As I pulled into the terminal, I was exhausted and ready to exit the bus. Fireproof was still playing on the TVs overhead, and I couldn't leave fast enough. It was a short taxi ride to the hotel I had picked in downtown Panama City. I quickly learned that in 2012, almost anywhere outside Panama City was difficult to find an affordable place to stay with solid Wi-Fi to perform my work duties. This was frustrating as I hit wall after wall, all the while residing in a Marriott, this was not how I envisioned life in Panama would be.

After 3 days of continued failed attempts at finding a suitable home, it was time to decide to move on or return to Nicaragua. I honestly think the thought of another 26-hour bus ride back to Nicaragua with Fireproof playing nonstop was the key factor in deciding to move onward. But to where was the question? I was at the end of Central America, so this meant I would have to fly to my next destination. Looking at a map, the logical choices were Columbia or Ecuador. I left it up to a coin toss to determine my fate. The coin landed on heads, so Ecuador it was. That day, I booked a flight to leave in 3 days.

This decision left me with limited time to tour Panama City. I am not huge on tourist spots, but the one place I wanted to see was the Panama Canal. It didn't feel right to be there without seeing this engineering marvel, and I am glad I did. The canal was extremely impressive, and they had grandstands you could sit in to watch the massive ships pass through the initial two steps of the Mira Flores Locks. These two locks manage to raise ships 54 feet higher as they let the water rush in. The ships traveling through the locks must surrender their boats to a Panamanian captain (to include raising the Panamanian Flag on their masts). Many ships were huge and had very little leeway on either side as they steered through the canal, so the captain piloting the ships must be certified and skilled in navigating the tight canal locks.

The remainder of the days spent in Panama consisted of getting in some short runs along the waterfront and starting the preparation for the next stop in Quito, Ecuador. Research showed that the Wi-Fi in Quito was fast and reliable. This put me at ease since the pace I was going for was a minimum of one month per country. This pace would allow me enough time to settle and fully absorb the culture instead of just being in a vacation mode. I wanted to be immersed in the culture and was determined to stay in Quito for a minimum of one month. Upon landing in Quito, I instantly knew that a month there wouldn't be enough and would require me to adjust my schedule yet again.

Ecuador

As the plane was approaching Quito, the capital of Ecuador, I could see how large the city was and was reassured in the coin toss that had me choose this country. This would be my third country to call home for the foreseeable future.

Having been in Panama and Nicaragua with such little luggage, it was important to keep my packing to a minimum. This wasn't very difficult as the countries I had been visiting were tropical and very warm. I was confident Ecuador would be the same, as Quito was on the equator. Where could it be warmer than the equator? It turns out a lot of places could be much warmer. Quito was indeed on the equator, but it is also nestled in the Andean foothills at an elevation of around 10,000 feet above sea level. To add to that, it was August, so technically it was winter there (although the ambient temperature doesn't fluctuate very much).

Quito is a beautiful city with even more beautiful people. As the cab dropped me off, I was still over a mile from my hotel I had booked for the next month. The issue was that it was Sunday and the roads all going into Mariscal Foch (the city center) were closed and open only for bicyclists. Since I had been running almost daily in Nicaragua and had dropped some weight, I slapped one backpack on my back and one on my front and thought I'd get a nice run in as I made my way towards my hotel. This would help warm me up, too, since I was only in shorts and a t-shirt. That was another bad idea. I quickly learned that running at 10,000 feet of elevation wiped me out quickly. I think I made it 4 minutes before my hands were on my knees and the packs were sliding off my back. This, I am certain, was quite a scene for the locals who were casually riding their bicycles up and down the main street, staring at me as I felt like I was about to die.

Upon arriving successfully at the hotel I first confirmed the Wi-Fi to ensure this location was suitable for my day job. The connectivity worked great, but there was just one hitch. The Wi-Fi knocked you offline every 60 minutes. To me, this was a simple fix of logging off of it before each conference call so that it wouldn't force me off mid-stream during the calls. That was easy enough and worked perfectly without any problems.

Once settled in Quito, a wave of relief fell over me, knowing that I could relax and focus fully on work for the next month. That was important as there had just been a reorganization, and I had a new manager. Three months into traveling through Central and now South America, and still no one knew I was anywhere but Boston, nor did they ask. I was fine with that and made it a point to keep it quiet, but not because I wasn't performing. I was performing and at an elevated level, but I thought someone might be upset if they knew I was doing this and would put the kybosh on it. I wasn't about to let that happen, so I took steps (to include disabling my social media accounts to ensure my secret wouldn't get out). I had a trustworthy peer, so I let him know, just in case there was a volcanic eruption or political uprising, so they could let my manager know that "Mike may not make it to work today." Of course, the chances of that were slim, so it was time to settle into a productive routine. I knew Ecuador might be my new home for longer than I had planned, and I had no problem with that at all.

Feeling confident that Quito, Ecuador, would work out for the foreseeable future, I wanted to begin absorbing the culture as I did in Nicaragua. One of the best ways of doing this was to start taking Spanish lessons. A great thing I learned about Ecuador almost instantly is that they spoke Spanish much more slowly than in Central America, where I was frequently lost by the lightning speed with which they spoke. This would be the perfect place to take lessons, where I could retain and practice speaking Spanish constantly as I went about my daily routines. Fortunately, there was an excellent Spanish school just two blocks from my hotel so that I could attend classes during lunch. It felt great to take steps towards integrating into this incredible culture.

I adjusted to a routine of work and Spanish lessons during the weekdays, and on weekends, I would explore local hikes and rainforests. I was almost at the base of Cotopaxi. Cotopaxi is technically is the highest mountain in the world, as it is on the equator and bulges out more than Mt. Everest (if you're one of those rare people who believe the Earth is round).

With my weekday schedule and routine defined by Spanish classes and runs to increase my tolerance at the high elevation, I returned to being successful at my day job as a project manager. I was doing my best to conserve my vacation days for the next country, Weekends were the only time to explore the surrounding areas of Quito in more depth. This, of course, had to include a trip to the equator.

The equator was just a short train ride from Quito. I fully understood it would be a total tourist trap, but where else would I have this opportunity to jump on both sides of the line like an idiot? It felt almost mandatory to do so. When preparing to leave, I saw an indigenous tour that brought me into the Andes Mountains and included a 4-mile round trip hike. As I boarded the bus, figuring I would be solo on this trip, three Germans jumped into the bus, reeking of BO with nothing but a tiny backpack each held. As we were dropped off and began the hike into the Andes, I started a conversation with one of them who didn't have shoes. It seems someone stole his shoes in Chile while playing soccer with some kids, and he decided not to purchase another pair. It was also interesting that the only items in his backpack were a machete, a journal, and his passport. I was instantly intrigued. These guys were minimalists to another level. Coming from me, that is quite an extreme statement.

As we reached the summit of our hike, there was an overlook that peered down into a small village in the valley of the Andes. It was abundantly clear that time hadn't touched or changed this hidden village. As the guide ushered us in a half circle for him to sing and give thanks to all the beauty around us, the German I had befriended was fidgeting around and produced a marijuana joint and sparked it up while the guide was deep into his singing. However, some would see this as very disrespectful. The guide seemed to relish the smoke that emitted from the joint. This German represented full freedom to me. He was probably the most carefree person I have ever met in my life, and most of the people I surround myself with are pretty carefree, so this guy now has another title to add to minimalist in my eyes.

As my Quito adventure continued, I settled into a routine. One of my better work habits is writing a to-do list over the weekend for work tasks with dates. This has helped me not only in my organization, but also in the prioritization of tasks to stay ahead of any deadlines my team or I are responsible for. Usually, I write this list on a Friday afternoon when I am in good spirits and tend to over commit, yet hold myself accountable for these deadlines. With hiking most weekends in Quito and exploring, I found myself not having written out my list, and it was Sunday afternoon with no plans.

I chose to go to a dark Irish bar in the heart of Quito to write my list. As I ordered a cold beer and began outlining my objectives for the week, I didn't notice that the bar became less and less crowded. It was now about 4:30 PM, and I was alone in the bar with three beautiful Ecuadorian females. The bartender began pulling the shades down and locking the doors. With no idea where this was going, I thought I would order another beer before the bartender asked me to go home. It seems in Quito, if you are IN the bar when they close, you can stay. It didn't take long for the Ecuadorians to invite me over, and I quickly decided my task list was completed for the day. I was in love with Quito, Ecuador!

As the weeks flew by, my time was filled with hiking, work, and immersing myself in the culture of this beautiful country I now called home. My frustration with work problems melted away as soon as I left the hotel every afternoon to meet new friends and partake in all the activities throughout the city of Quito.

Entering Week 4 in Quito, I began to feel in the groove enough to venture forward. Although Ecuador has endless activities and places to explore, I was saving my vacation for the next country that I wanted to become even more immersed in. There would be no coin toss for this next stop, as my soul has yearned to visit this country for years. Peru!

Peru

Feeling sad departing Ecuador, as it was quickly becoming a home for me where I was very comfortable, I boarded a flight to Lima, Peru, to take in a new corner of the world. Peru has always felt like the pinnacle of South America. Even though I had never been there and knew very little about it, there was a calling for me to embrace this country. In fact, this resonated so strongly with me that I purposely cut a lot out of Ecuador to conserve my vacation for Peru.

After only two days in Lima, I quickly learned this wasn't the Peru I was looking for. It was just a large city, and cities weren't where I would find the culture and experiences that would help me grow. Knowing this, I booked a 12-hour bus ride to Cusco. Surprisingly, I clearly hadn't learned my lesson from the Nicaragua to Panama bus ride. Still, I figured the chances of a repeat performance of Fireproof being played nonstop were pretty slim.

Falling asleep on the overnight bus ride while gazing out the window at the ocean and expansive desert of Lima, and then awakening to the massive vistas of the Andes Mountain range, wasn't a bad way to travel.

I did, however, have a killer headache upon arrival in Cusco. Wasting no time, I found a cab to drive me to my Airbnb, where I could relax for a bit. The host noticed I wasn't looking too healthy and made me some tea. Within an hour, I felt great. Turns out the elevation of approximately 12,000 feet, along with some minor dehydration, was the cause of my headache. The tea she gave me had coca leaves in it. These leaves are not only a cure for altitude sickness, but they soon became a replacement for my morning coffee.

As with Ecuador, it didn't take long for me to get into a productive work and exercise routine. My lunchtime became a break from technology, and technology which was replaced by runs through the city of Cusco. It was beyond magical. This place was a perfect balance of culture and history with some color mixed in. During my runs, I noticed there were always girls dressed in full Peruvian dresses walking around with what looked like baby llamas. It turns out you can hold and pet a baby llama for like three sole (about $1 USD). I like baby llamas. I mean, who doesn't? So, every night during my evening strolls, I ensured I had a few soles to give them and looking back, I probably spent more on pictures with the baby llamas than I did on dinners.

Obtaining Peruvian soles for currency was as simple as going to an ATM. One problem that seemed to constantly arise was that if the money was not in pristine condition, the stores would refuse to take it. This refusal was often after a long huddle of the store's employees and management to confirm that the currency was too badly damaged to accept. After a few frustrating days of this, I happened to visit Paddy's Pub. It is the world's 2nd highest Irish pub. I noticed they took my currency no matter what condition it was in. Perfect! Adding Paddy's Pub to my daily itinerary to launder money for baby llama petting was an outstanding solution. The world was coming together quite nicely for Paddy's, the llamas, and me.

It took no time for me to fall in love with Cusco. The people were wonderful and every weekend there was some event in the square. It was easy to jump on any random bus and end up in hidden ruins, AND there were baby llamas everywhere to hang out with. My work performance was improving even more than in Ecuador. At this time, no one knew I was anywhere but Boston and would occasionally ask, "How's the weather up there in Boston?" which I would quickly Google and reply ", Meh, 60s cloudy, it's Boston, ya know?" I never lied to them about where I was; they just never thought to ask, and even if I had told them, they never would have believed me.

With my morale greatly improved and in a productive routine, I was convinced Cusco would be my new home for as long as possible. Even better, my Airbnb host's son was a travel agent. Perfect. We met for dinner, and he helped me set up plans to travel to different parts of the country every weekend, and many became 4-day weekend trips, allowing me not to rush and really absorb the beauty and culture in remote areas that many would never see or experience. These trips included Machu Picchu, Lake Titicaca (like I would miss out on going to not only the highest alpine lake on Earth, but endless jokes based on the name, "Lake Titicaca"). After three weeks of adapting to Cusco, it was time to explore deeper in order to really take a bite out of the surrounding areas that would yield some of my greatest memories and travel experiences to date.

Peru 2 (Machu Picchu)

Peru is most famously known for one of the 7 Wonders of the World. What's frustrating is that, like national parks in the United States, whoever declares things a "Wonder of the World" keeps adding more to the list, or, in this case, with the 7 Wonders, they change them. Absolutely one of my life's objectives is to hit all 7 Wonders. Machu Picchu is and should always remain in that highly respected list of these magnificent artifacts of humanity's past.

Getting to Machu Picchu isn't easy, even if you are living in Peru. I feel the best way is to hike the Inca Trail over three or four days to arrive at this city deep in the Andes. One of the biggest issues with my whimsical lifestyle is that it is difficult to plan too far in advance. To reserve a spot to hike the Inca Trail (at the time in 2012) was about four months. In Huber travel years, that is equal to about two years, so that option was out. The more touristy way to arrive is via a train with a glass roof. Compared to my past bus rides, it was heaven (there were no showings of Fireproof on this ride).

The train pulled into Aquas Calientes. Aquas Calientes is the small town nestled deep in the Andes at the base of Machu Picchu. Almost instantly, I was filled with energy. I don't know if it was energy from the ancient civilization that once resided here, or if it was being at the lower elevation of 7,000 feet as compared to the 12,000 feet where I had been living.

The following day, I was up early to catch the first bus up to Machu Picchu. The bus ride was filled with hairpin turns with quick glimpses of one of the 7 Wonders. I had my face pressed into the cold bus window, awaiting each new view around every corner. Upon arrival, I stopped at the kiosk just outside the park entrance to load up on water since a full day of hiking was on the itinerary.

Once entering the ruins and taking some time to... yes, hang out with the llamas...the realization hit me that I had two full days in this mesmerizing ancient city! I noticed people would unload from buses, do a quick photo in that iconic spot we all have seen in every travel magazine, have an hour or so to explore the ruins, and then they were off. What's funny is that the angle is not even of Mt. Machu Picchu, but of Huayna Picchu. Having two full days here would allow me the opportunity to summit both mountains and enjoy the area to its fullest.

The first day, I decided I would climb the higher and much less visited of the two summits. Mt. Machu Picchu towers approximately 1,800 feet above the Inca city below. This should have been a more strenuous hike, but with being 4,000 feet lower in elevation, the energy from these powerful ruins, and a solid reserve of coca leaves, the mountain was a fairly easy climb. With so few people along the trail (I was one of the first in the park, and many were just there for the photo ops), the trail was pretty much mine for the morning.

After the hike and with the coca leaves leaving my system, it was time for a siesta. I wandered throughout the ruins until I found a hidden room and climbed atop the walls in the sun and snoozed for a bit until some new friends awoke me. Marmots. The little guys were scampering throughout the ruins and occasionally would knock off rocks loud enough to jostle me awake. The day couldn't have been more perfect.

Day Two in the ruins was a similar routine, with me catching the first shuttle of the morning. Plans for this day were to summit Huayna Picchu and then hike down behind the mountain to almost the same elevation as my base of Aquas Caliente, but on the other side of the mountain. This area had no one in it. It was a steep trail. In one hike, it left the Andes Mountains and descended into a rain forest that felt like no one had visited in centuries. It wasn't nearly as large as the main city on top of the mountain, but it had a few structures overrun with jungle growth. The difference in climate on this short and steep hike was amazing. After returning, it was time for another nap and a few more short hikes along portions of the Inca Trail before returning to the shuttle to bring me back to Aquas Calientes.

With life always seeming so busy and the pressure to constantly move and go, it was more than nice to be able to allocate so much time here and fully embrace every part of this city. Few people have this opportunity, and the ones that do, tend to rush through it so quickly that they don't allow themselves to feel the mystical energy that emits from this city in the clouds of Peru called Machu Picchu.

Peru 3 (Lake Titicaca)

No trip to Peru can be complete without a journey to Lake Titicaca. It is the largest alpine lake on the planet at an elevation of 12,500 feet, and the lifestyle of those who live on the lake is just fascinating. This huge lake is nestled in a giant basin between two of the Andean mountain ranges and extends across the border to Bolivia. And yes, it has a funny name. There was no way I was going to miss this place, even though it was quite a distance from my home base in Cusco.

Having planned to use all my vacation time while in Peru, it wasn't too difficult to load up on my work early in the week and take a four-day weekend to knock out Lake Titicaca (did I mention it has a funny name?). Allowing four days would provide me with enough time to take a leisurely tour bus to this region of Peru, get some hikes and tourist attractions in along the way, and then return on an overnight bus on Sunday. This would assure (hopefully) that I would make it to work on time on Monday morning. Instilling project management principles usually results in a successful outcome. To me, the planning of a project or a vacation followed the same rigid processes. Of course, the vacation ones always had a few surprises along the way that I would have to adjust to, but that's part of the fun.

The bus ride was filled with incredible beauty, with stops at local markets and panoramic mountain views that had me saying to myself, "Wow, I am in the Andes!" over and over again. Out of all the bus rides I'd been on, this was by far the most pleasant. I was used to the altitude, there were no Kirk Cameron movies, and I had made a special tea to enhance the ride (See the chapter on San Pedro). The entire ride was an extremely joyful 8 hours where I had an opportunity to meet two wonderful girls from Japan and we are still friends to this day.

Feeling beyond happy but tired, I finally pulled into the lakeside city of Pulmo, Peru. This first day here would be relaxing and adjusting to the world I had just entered. A giant golden condor statue on a steep hill above the city provided a sense of calm as you explored a large market area. The market made for great people watching while having some coca tea and even a coca beer. The coca beer was interesting as it provided you with a buzz and also a rush of energy from the coca at the same time. It almost reminded me of my Jager bomb days in Boston. Thankfully for the people of Pulmo, I didn't take it that far.

The next day, I joined a boat tour and sailed out to many of the man-made islands. These islands were floating and made of dried totora, a type of papyrus the local population harvested from the lake marshes. The people are known as the Ura. The islands are fairly large, some of them over an acre or more in size. There were stores, restaurants, and even cafes on some of the islands.

The islands were surprisingly stable and didn't rock as I stepped onto them. When talking to one of the Ura (and speaking as well as I could in Spanish), I asked how they made the islands once they gathered the papyrus. It was a constant cycle of drying the papyrus, bundling it, and tying it to the upper part of the island. He showed me a hole cut into the center of one of the islands. It looked like a hole you would ice fish through, and it was about 3 feet wide. The hole was large enough to see the bottom reeds starting to decay and fall back into the water. It was a constant process to keep their "land" from being swallowed by the lake. Many of the Ura, not much more than a mile offshore, hardly ever returned to the mainland shores of Pulmo. They much preferred their isolated yet tightly knit community on the lake, where life was simple.

The city of Pulmo was so different from both the Amazon jungle and where I lived in Cusco. The more I explored Peru, the more diverse and mystical it became. Sunday was a relaxing day with more coca beer and local foods with my new Japanese friends.

As the sun began to set, it was time to find my way back to the bus depot and board the redeye that would return me to Cusco. It didn't take too long for me to peacefully fall asleep on the bus. I didn't wake up until the bus entered Cusco. It was a short taxi ride to my home and just in time to lead my first conference call of the day. Still bleary-eyed and having a buzz from the weekend (and the coca beer), my workday progressed as though the trip was just a dream. It was an adventure I wanted to share with my co-workers, but they wouldn't understand, as they were still under the assumption I was living in my condo in Boston. Throughout the day, I wondered if and when I would ever return to Boston.

Peru 4 (It's Probably Time to Head Back)

Balancing life is rarely easy. It seems there is something always out of sync, be it work, health, or a loved one in need of help. Peru is one of those rare times in my life where I and everything surrounding me seemed to be in perfect harmony. I was coming up on six weeks living in Cusco, and the adventures seemed endless from my home base there. I was making a ton of new friends, but with Cusco being so much more of a tourist town, these new connections were always short lived. Surely now it's different with so many Westerners living abroad and working remotely, but being a pioneer of this lifestyle in 2012, missing a community began to set in. Not so much on the weekends as I was too busy, but during the weekdays, a void started to drain me.

The decision to make the long journey back to the United States was not an easy one. It took so long to get to where I was. I even had built connections for my next planned move to La Paz, Bolivia. I was running very low on vacation time, and everything I wanted to see in Bolivia was a multiple-day bus ride. Buffering in unknowns (such as a bus breaking down in the middle of nowhere) was necessary. I would be city bound in La Paz, and I don't think they had as many baby llamas to pet, so Bolivia didn't feel right on any level.

The last week in Peru was a much deeper experience (I didn't even know it could get deeper than where I had been). Every moment I was out felt much more special, knowing that my time was short in this magical place. There was a lot to do in my Cusco backyard that hadn't been explored. My focus had been on visiting remote areas such as Lake Titicaca (I had to say it again), rather than exploring the wonders closer to my home.

My final week in Peru was filled with exploring local points of interest, such as the San Pedro market, where there were all kinds of foods, drinks, and potions that most Westerners will never see or smell (be thankful you are missing the smell part). The market consisted of endless types of food. Many of these foods seemed to be pulled straight out of an Indiana Jones movie. It wasn't strange to see Guinea pigs' necks being snapped, and then the animal being tossed into a boiling pot, gutted, and grilled. Other items included horse heads, pig heads, and snakes in water jars. This market was a plethora of sensory overload. Usually, I would visit it to pick up a bag of coca leaves for about 30 cents and some of my "special" tea mix.

Somehow, I still managed to find time to do silly things with downtime during the weekdays. My last Sunday in Peru, it poured, and being bored, I was searching the apartment for something to eat while watching TV. I found in the back of the refrigerator a beer pitcher that

I had filled with coca leaves a week or so prior, and added a bottle of white wine. The wine had absorbed the coca leaves and turned the wine a dark yellow. Being that this chapter was coming to an end, I thought it would be the perfect day to partake in this concoction. Who knows, maybe it would have similar effects to the coca beer. I drank the entire pitcher. The coca-infused wine just had this bitter, earthy taste that I really enjoyed. Like the coca beer, it provided a jolt of energy with a nice light buzz that assisted me in packing and wrapping up my life in the Andean city of Cusco.

With the coca wine buzzing inside my head, a bigger question emerged: Where was I to live upon returning to the United States? My Boston condo was rented for another five months, so that option was out. I was not sure if it was the wine or the fact that this change may not be as simple as I had anticipated. Throughout my travels around Central and South America, it always seemed that if things went south, I could return to the United States. Being so preoccupied in the moment during my travels, however, I never designed a fallback plan aside from boarding a return flight.

As the week came to an end, I was now boarding that flight. I was not, however, in too big a rush. It felt right to instead return to Nicaragua for a couple of weeks and ease my way north, and see my dogs. While I was there, Hurricane Sandy hit and knocked out power throughout the Northeast. That morning, as I watched the news, I had a decision to make: Do I power up the laptop and be the only person in the Northeast who showed up for work, or do I continue with the "I am in Boston" charade?

I chose Option A, deciding that I was on my way back and had been outperforming most of my peers for six months throughout five countries. My coworkers immediately questioned how I had internet, and my answer was, "I saw there was a hurricane, so being remote, I chose to go south to avoid it." Not a lie, but not totally forthcoming. If I had replied with "I am working in the jungles of Nicaragua", no one would have believed me (this came up months later, and no one did).

After the two weeks, it was time to fully return to Boston to regroup. It was a rainy November day when I touched down at Logan. I weighed 30 pounds less, and mentally I was even lighter. I still had no plan regarding what to do once I left the aircraft at Logan. My car was at a friend's house. My Ducati was at my parent's home in Maine. Before I had even cleared through Customs and Immigration, though, I knew this was no longer the place that called to me. The reentry shock into the United States was too much. I was swelling up with tears knowing it was now time to make the hard decision to leave New England, but where would I go, as winter was beginning?

Victoria, British Columbia

Landing back in Boston mid-November, the only thing perfect was the weather. Perfect for hypothermia, that is. It didn't take long in the cold and damp environment for me to realize that this would not be a suitable location for winter, especially after having been in tropical climates for the past 8 months. However, the decision not to stay was an easy one; where to actually move opened up an entirely new set of questions—this part of the journey I had not planned for very well, or at all. It was time to pull out some maps and just as I had done in South America, find a solution to the problem I now faced: Where would be my new home?

I wasn't a big fan of the southeastern states and hadn't really explored many of the western ones. Since the gray, damp weather wasn't something I wanted to deal with, deciding to choose the Pacific Northwest probably wasn't one of my better ideas, but I knew it wouldn't be as cold in that area. I was still feeling the culture shock of returning to the United States. After living in South America the busy and stressful vibe of the United States wasn't tolerable.

Having narrowed the region down, the next step was to pinpoint a spot. Looking at maps, I noticed a rather large land mass not too far off the coast of Seattle and Vancouver. It was Vancouver Island, and the capital of British Columbia, Victoria. This seemed like a perfect place to call home until I could find a better location.

After a quick and uneventful drive cross country, I was at the ferry terminal in Port Angeles, Washington, about to embark on another out of country adventure. As soon as the Blackball ferry pulled into Victoria Harbor I knew this would be a fun place. The inner harbour had a number of float planes landing and taking off. The Victoria Clipper (a high speed catamaran) was there, and tugboat looking water taxis buzzed around the much larger Blackball ferry like mosquitoes around an elephant. The entire inner harbor was just so alive.

Upon disembarking from the ferry, there was a bit of a wait going through Canadian Customs, where they scanned my passport and I confidently assured them I was visiting only for a week. In all honesty, I really didn't have much of an idea about the length of my visit, as my planning (much like today) is almost nonexistent. The next step was to find a place to stay for a week or so until I could get my bearings and determine if I wanted to stay here longer. Having just driven over 3,000 miles, I wasn't in much of a rush to leave.

It didn't take too long for me to find a cool hotel that allowed for longer stays near the center of town. The hotel was a great selling point, not only for the location, but also because it had what was probably the best Chinese restaurant in the basement. And if that wasn't enough, there was the best dive bar attached to the hotel. Even with the rainy weather that lowered my morale, the restaurant and the bar gave refuge and let me refill my endorphins. This place would do nicely.

One of the best ways I've found to learn a new city is to go for long runs, get lost, and then learn the area. Frequently, during these runs, I would find someone running the same pace and strike up a conversation. This happened on one of my first days in Victoria. I kept pace with a man a few years older than me, and as our conversation continued, I jokingly explained I was here working remotely, possibly quite illegally, and we both had a good laugh. Our finishing point was just after we crossed a bridge, when I introduced myself and he did the same. "Nice to meet you, Mike," he said. "I'm Dean, the Mayor of Victoria, but you can call me Mayor Dean." He handed me a business card and invited me to visit his office if I needed anything. My jaw was on the ground. I expected Canadian Mounties or Immigration to jump from around the corner. This, of course, didn't happen (it was Canada and they are very warm people, even to illegal visitors like me).

Despite the weather being a bit gray (this is to be expected in December in the Pacific Northwest), this island was a great choice. Within two weeks, it was obvious this was to be my home at least through the winter months (unless Mayor Dean disapproved). It was time to find a longer term rental on a month to month lease. Even that type of lease was quite a commitment for me. Even more so, since I probably wasn't allowed to be in Canada for more than 90 days, as per their immigration law. This would be another problem for future Mike to deal with, which he did successfully. It was now time to start exploring my new home and see what there was to offer this American traveler and digital nomad.

With all the traveling I had been so happy, that I didn't even notice how smoothly my projects that I was managing were going. Several directors and upper management did. They recommended I interview for a management position. The interview process went very smoothly until they raised a concern that I was in Boston and my team would be in Seattle. Now, over the past year or so, I have never lied to anyone about my location. I just didn't disclose it. It seemed either they were one question away from finding out or I was one answer ahead of them, but I never lied to them. So when they mentioned my Boston location being a possible hindrance, I decided to just let it all out. I informed them I had been living in Central and South America and was now on Vancouver Island in Canada. As you can imagine, there was quite a pause after that, followed by some laughter as if I was joking with them. The laughter ended when I shared my laptop screen and began showing photos to them from all over, including my dogs in Nicaragua, lamas in Peru, and pretty much everywhere I had been. If I remember correctly, they said something to the effect, "We've seen enough, just take the management position, Huber, and you will be allowed to travel as you please". I ultimately was offered and accepted the position.

Returning to the USA

I lived and worked in the beautiful rainforest island town of Victoria, British Columbia. Still, I had noticed the past couple of times returning from my work trips to Seattle that the Canadian Immigration people started to take notice of me and were more than aware that the stories I was feeding them weren't true (they could see my entry/exit dates, and those dates did NOT track with what I was telling them). During one of the last times I crossed the border, I was pulled aside. They ran my Massachusetts driver's license, and the agent quickly stated, "You're a long way from home son." I provided my normal reply by pointing at my backpack: No, sir. My home is right there. He didn't find it funny (they never do). He returned my IDs and had me move through Customs without further issue.

It was definitely time to return to the United States. It didn't take too long over the next week to pack up, deflate the leaky air mattress I had been sleeping on for 8 months, and place the Goodwill furniture on the corner. The furniture and I shared the same situation; we were both looking for our next home. Loading everything into the car was the final step before getting on the Tsawwassen Ferry. This ferry would bring me to Vancouver. It was a short and uneventful 3-hour drive to my new residence in Seattle, Washington.

Victoria was one of the very few places that made me cry when I left. I had a beautiful eight months living there and felt so fortunate that I was not only able to experience this island and the great people who live there, but that I was able to stay for so long. It is one of the few places I have lived that I proudly called my home.

I was back in the United States after a year and a half. It was time to get an actual apartment and furniture that wasn't from Goodwill. Belltown in Seattle seemed to be a no-brainer as far as a location. There were tons of bars and restaurants, it was next to the Olympic Sculpture Park, and the Victoria Clipper was right there (if I felt the urge to jump back to Victoria on the high-speed catamaran). Maybe the coolest part of Belltown was that my apartment was in the shadow of the Space Needle.

The one big lesson I learned in my vagabond, digital nomad travels is that it is much easier to get back on the wheel than it is to exit it. Getting an apartment and having my furniture sent from Boston was easy. Leaving the wheel required a ton of planning and preparation. It took months to downsize, find a storage space for my vehicles, rent my condo, etc. The tasks seemed to never end when I prepared to leave the wheel, and as I completed each task, I found myself constantly questioning my decision as I counted down to Day 0.

I was now a Seattle resident. Over the past 18 months, I left from the start of I-90 near Fenway Park to the end of the same road at Safeco Field. It would have only been a 3,000 mile trip on I-90, but I took the longest route possible by meandering through five countries. I was anxious to meet new friends and see how being back on the wheel would treat me, and more importantly, how I would adjust to this old lifestyle I had left.

Digital Nomad: The Seattle Years

I wasn't thrilled the first few months in Seattle after having moved from Victoria. The timing of my move didn't help since it was at the end of summer when the sun almost totally gives way to the gloomy gray clouds. It wasn't so much that it rained there, but you absolutely could feel less energy around you due to a serious lack of vitamin D in everyone's system. Nonetheless, I was here and had signed a one year lease in a high-rise in the Seattle neighborhood of Belltown, so I had to make the best of it.

It didn't take too long to feel closed in living in the city. Seattle isn't a big city, but what was missing was the nature that had engulfed and spoken to me over the past year. My "office," which I went in maybe once every few weeks to meet the team for coffee or happy hour, was in Bellevue. I am usually not one to badmouth areas, but instead I like to look at the positive side and its attributes. In Bellevue, I couldn't find any. It was a suburban plastic city with nothing but cookie cutter restaurants and bars. It was like The Truman Show, but with a "keep up with the Jones" mentality. Everyone had expensive cars and would even move parking spaces to flaunt the material items they had become slaves to. When asking them what they did on the weekend, it usually entailed going to Costco and dinner at a Chili's or Cheesecake Factory to wrap up a day at the mall.

Thankfully, I rode my Ducati Monster M1100 out of Maine. This became the best way to leave the beaten path and explore the state of Washington, and boy, did I explore it! The learning curve was a quick one in discovering incredible roads and remote camping areas that most people didn't dare to explore. There were no Chili's out on the Olympic Peninsula, and that was fine with me.

Once again, every weekend was like a vacation for me as I explored Washington. When I went into the office, my peers would gather to hear about where I went over the weekend and what I had experienced. There were numerous challenging hikes, remote beach camping on the

Olympic Peninsula, motorcycle rides through the Cascades, numerous volcanoes, and countless treasures I discovered by talking to fellow hikers and riders. I was starting to love Washington. The diversity inspired me to explore the region, and it was a rare weekend when I stayed in Seattle.

It didn't take long before I got over the fear of city life, built a circle of great friends, and became fully acclimated to living in Belltown. The weekends involved traveling through the state or up to Vancouver, BC, and weekdays I spent in coffee shops and bars with my new friends. Life became pretty routine (anything routine was odd for me), but it was enjoyable.

One of the coolest things I loved about Seattle is how dog friendly the city is. For years, they had a dog that rode the city bus with a bus pass to the local dog park. Also, dogs are not only allowed in most bars but actually sit at the bar, and the bartender provides a water dish and treats for them. I have been in bars where, at times, there are more dogs than people. This just added to my feelings for this city.

Although after almost three years living in the Seattle area and exploring most of its secrets, there were a few moments that told me it was time to return to my nomadic lifestyle. One was during a Seattle Seahawks playoff game. It was on TV, and I went out on my tiny balcony to get some air. I looked around at all the high rise apartments next to me, and EVERY television was on the same channel, watching the same thing. It was a scene out of George Orwell's 1984. It freaked me out, and that was one of the seeds that began in nudging me to move on. The other was the gray skies. I was beginning to become depressed from a lack of vitamin D, and no matter how many supplements I took, I could feel I was sinking into a depressive abyss. My parents, always ones to come up with creative solutions, sent me a mood light for Christmas. It didn't help.

That one final Seattle winter only provided the city with twenty hours of sun from mid-October until May. I decided to take action. I threw the mood light in the trash and devised a plan to leave Seattle and spend a month in Montana. Little did I know that this decision would morph into a series of life-changing events.

The Ride

"I am slowly dying every day I am here."

It was April 2017, and that was the thought that kept going through my head. I was living in Seattle, and it was one of the grayest winters in Pacific Northwest history. According to meteorological scientists, there had been only twenty hours of sunlight from October to May. I was working remotely; a strange, novel existence that in a young and lighter life was referred to as telecommuting. To work remotely is to live semi-detached from the rest of society. At times, it feels as though you are physically invisible to the world; literally, a digital personality. Of course, this was before the global pandemic came in and made remote work the new normal for those of us fortunate enough to have a job. I had begun losing motivation in my work and in most other aspects of life, and it wasn't just the weather. Maybe it was the fact that I wore the same ratty Boston University hoodie every day that winter and ate Shin Ramen for two of my three meals a day. Maybe it was that the people I saw in the streets and places I frequented seemed to be as isolated and disconnected as I was feeling at the time.

Looking back on those gray, empty Seattle days, I realize now that the need for freedom and openness was what finally forced me to make such a drastic change. I needed a hard reset of my current mindset and environment, one that would revolve around my passion for riding motorcycles. I wanted to take the chess game that had become my life and forearm swipe the whole thing across the room. Kind of like the Jack Nicholson diner scene in Five Easy Pieces. So that is exactly what I decided to do.

New Game

I had chosen to put the Jet City in my rearview mirror and travel the country on my Ducati Monster M1100. This torquey little machine had a dry clutch with a stiff pull, which made a beautiful "clack clack clack" sound. It reminded me of a WWII P-51 Mustang heading into a dog fight alone, against a squadron of Messerschmidts. I loved my Monster. We had seven good years together, feeling the wind in my hair and the angry vibes of the 1100 CC v-twin engine on two-lane roads all over this amazing country. I even camped off with this sleek little machine during a memorable ride down the coast to San Francisco. To me, the Ducati Monster M1100 is everything that a motorcycle should be—nothing extra, and nothing less. In fact, the only thing that the bike wasn't fit for was the journey I was about to take.

The Plan

The high level plan was to head east on I-90, blaze through Eastern Washington and Idaho in one go, not stopping until I hit the unadulterated freedom of open space called Montana. I would camp every chance I could in the open air majesty of perhaps our greatest treasure: America's National Forests. I planned to visit National Parks and stop to see every UFO landing site and giant ball of string that caught my eye. Most importantly, I would make sure that my thirst for the road on a fossil fuel burning two-wheeler was quenched daily. I would live in Airbnbs during the week, feeding my pencil thin bank account by logging in to my nine-to-five via laptop as an IT project manager. Although I did fine at my job, I had this unique perspective that work was a vehicle, a vehicle when pointed in the right direction and driven with the right intent, could be used to feed my hunger for riding, camping, and living life in a way that I would not regret when my last days arrived. Monday through Friday, I would continue to persevere in my career. Weekends, however, would be all mine. I intended to max each one out with the whistle of speed in my ears and a thick coating of dead insects on my face shield.

Seattle

The weather finally broke in May. I greeted the first rays of sun with squinted eyes, dangerously low vitamin D levels and a steaming cup of Starbucks which would be my last for a while. I loaded the Ducati with all my gear and took a step back to look things over. The packing list was dangerously minimal, yet the bike looked like something off of Sanford and Son. My gear was just too much for the journey I had planned on the Ducati.

I had to make a difficult decision that I had been stewing on for years. Some might call it an upgrade, some might call it the death of romance. Some might call it the end of the sexy and lyrical object worship and variable reliability that is the result of Italian design and engineering. That day… that fateful day, I traded my Ducati Monster in for a BMW GS1200.

Coming Out Of the Closet as an Adventure Rider

I now had the perfect bike for the adventure and the lifestyle I was about to launch into. I had no idea it would lead to an all-consuming life obsession that would take me over a 100,000 miles down every type of road imaginable on one excursion after another with no end in sight. When I departed Seattle on that first sunny day in May, I remember thinking, "I'll just cruise out to Montana tomorrow and get to know my new machine." My plan was light on detail, and I told myself I'd deal with that tomorrow. Besides, spring was in the air, and I had previously never spent more than a few days in Montana. At that time I was headed in the opposite direction and running on Red Bull and fumes, hunched over the Ducati's bars on a laser-focused run down the entire length of I-90 from Fenway Park in Boston to Seattle's Safeco Field.

That first day riding east was epic. As I left Seattle, I remembered the scene at the beginning of Easy Rider where Peter Fonda tossed his watch onto the desert sand as they kicked started their Vaughs and Hardy chops and blazed out eastward on their own adventure towards Mardi Gras. The day couldn't have tasted better. The smell of spring was thick in the cool morning air. The sky opened up as if to reassure me I had made the right choice and would be there to support and guide me in this liberating endeavor. The enormous evergreens of the coast became steadily shorter, fewer and farther between until they disappeared. They were replaced by tumbling sage and the open high desert of eastern Washington.

I don't know how fast I was going, but there was still a light mist coming off the Columbia River as I cut through a vicious crosswind on the bridge at Vantage. The traffic thinned out with every mile as the quiet machine practically rode itself eastbound. Spokane, Coer'D'Alene, Post Falls, Idaho… Well, hello, Montana! I rolled into Whitefish and stopped for my first full meal since I had left. It wasn't anything spectacular; a small brewery on the outskirts of town. I could have eaten a gas station bologna sandwich on stale bread and been just as happy. I had made that leap and had landed squarely outside the hamster wheel, looking in. It felt like coming home.

Montana is a rider's paradise. With a rough plan of spending 2 weeks in Whitefish, I would start by riding a road called Going to the Sun. This road is a rare and beautiful collection of breathtaking views in between sweeping switchback curves on good asphalt. The experience leaves you feeling unstoppable, while the occasional grizzly bear sighting reassures you that your place in the food chain is not always at the top.

Going to the Sun was a life-changing road on a bike that would prove life changing for me. The GS was silent compared to the Ducati. It had roll on power for the slow, steady grades of the continental divide. I sat up high and took in the wildflowers of spring and the smells of Ponderosa and Lodgepole pine as I changed the GS's road setting to sport mode, opened up the throttle and consumed mile after mile of sun baked highway.

At some point in mid-June, I lit out of Whitefish on Forest Service roads, starting to get a feel for what the GS and I were capable of together. Hunter S. Thompson famously said, 'The edge; the only ones who really know where it is, are the ones who have gone over.' There were several times on that ride when I had to dust myself off and pick up all 650 pounds of fully loaded GS before pointing her east and rolling on. A sort of cadence developed on those sandy mountain roads; drop the bike, swear a lot, cut the engine, swear some more, then pick her up, swear a bit more, onward and upward. It was all part of a steep learning curve that comes with all things worth doing. I learned that lesson one dropped a twenty-thousand-dollar German motorcycle at a time until the new car smell was all but washed off of her.

I was falling fast in love with my new bike and Montana, and soon after Whitefish, I decided to relocate to Missoula, where I began taking weekend trips out to experience some of America's most drooled over stretches of two lane blacktop. One of those American roads I will never forget is the Beartooth Highway. This highway stretches between Red Lodge and the Northeast Entrance to Yellowstone. If we set foot on Mars in my lifetime, I may volunteer to go.

Until that happens, I'll have the Beartooth Highway. It is a pristine lunar landscape that is literally without end, showcasing snowcapped peaks that go on forever to your left, right and center. The road going up Beartooth Pass is a chain of perfect hairpin switchbacks so consistent that after a few awkward peg scrapers, I was able to lean the big GS in with a confidence reminiscent of my old Ducati. I experienced seventy odd miles of rider's paradise on this first outing from my new Missoula basecamp. I finished the day dropping into Yellowstone. When Yellowstone is not choked off with Winnebagos and European tourists in black socks, it is truly one of the seven wonders I have personally experienced on two wheels. You can camp on a pristine prairie and share the view with the bison who will roam freely around you as you grill up a rib-eye from one of their close cousins and enjoy a well learned adult beverage in a tall can. This riding experience was something patently American; the stuff of childhood cowboy dreams and one I will never forget.

I hit Montana running, never planning more than two weeks, and I never really stopped. The ride has been something enviable to those who understand. I am currently writing this sitting in front of a warm fire on this chilly June day in Lake City, Colorado, with the GS unloaded and parked where I can keep an eye on her. I will spend a few more weeks tearing up the asphalt and dirt in this geographically diverse state before setting sights on my next challenge.

I try to avoid the news, but it's easy to see the world is spinning faster than ever these days. People seem to be polarizing more and more to where common ground is hard to find. In this unstable operating environment, you need to find a constant, a baseline; a solid rock that you can stand on, mentally and spiritually. Call it a ground-wire. For me, that constant is riding a motorcycle and the life that comes with it. Using the power of the ride to find common ground with people is one of the most magical talents I have learned to develop.

So, as I continue on my ride, I am reminded that balance on two wheels requires constant motion. And like my last listless, restless winter in Seattle, there can be great tension in standing still. I think of the balance sometimes when I am polishing off a tall can, watching the crackling campfire reflect off the GS's exhaust system, always parked close where I can keep an eye on her – after all, we are alone in a wild place. Now that I think about it, I'm pretty sure that's what keeps us together.

Psychedelic Adventures

Ketamine

So, usually in November and December, for an unknown reason, I fall into a deep depression. I am unsure of the root cause; no bad memories from childhood or any of that usual trauma you can point a finger at, but it gets bad. I pretty much suck to be around.

In 2019, I was traveling through Mexico and in an Airbnb in La Paz, and it just hit me so hard that I was pretty much deadlined for weeks. I am IN Mexico, living on a beach. There was no need or reason for me to be anything but ecstatic, but I was miserable, and it was dark mentally for me. The depression got so bad that my travel buddy had called my former platoon sergeant from the 82nd Airborne and relayed how much pain I was in. He called me that evening. While talking with him, I was drinking, he was drinking, I was drinking, he was drinking (We're paratroopers, we drink). He was clearly concerned, yet I just kept saying "I'm fine, I'm fine". Eventually, we ended the conversation, and my buddy went to bed. I proceeded to take out my hammock that had an extended 550 cord with knots every 5 feet and tried to hang myself off the balcony. I was too smashed to figure out the knots and gave up, frustrated. I couldn't even get that right. The next morning, I woke up on the ground, tangled up in the hammock (which I managed to put away before my buddy woke up). Definitely one of the sadder scenes I have had in my life.

I decided that the following year I want to get ahead of the depression and be proactive to avoid incidents like the one I just described. So I thought I would try ketamine, as some of my friends have used it with varying results.

I nervously showed up to the doctor's office, where they would administer the ketamine to me through an IV. Crying as I go over my depression history, suicidal thoughts, drinking habits, plant medicine experiences, and allergies. The doctor then puts on a National Geographic video with animals and natural beauty on her laptop and begins the IV drip. I lie back in a chair as she puts a weighted blanket on me (I know with psychedelics, you often feel cold). In about 20 minutes, I begin to feel the ketamine. It's like a morphine tingly high, but soon it becomes difficult to speak, my tongue and lips feel swollen, and slowly I blast off into another dimension.

As this happens, I could hear that sound that tells you that you're going on a journey, that loud humming mixed with the sound of your Father tuning in the radio and hearing different sounds of static, tones, music, and voices until he finds the station he likes to listen to with Paul Harvey. I remember exhaling deeply several times. The doctor stayed there and responded, "Breathe, Michael, you are in a safe environment" I asked if there was music playing, and there was from the video. I really began to take off. I hear the heart monitor beep a few times and think, "shit, I may flat line", and I quickly change thoughts to not go down a dark path. I am outside my body; there is just a small light in a different dimension floating around, which I know I am the light. I had my eyes closed for much of it, but would occasionally open them to see I was still in the office. I couldn't feel my hands when I was moving my fingers and became concerned, but then "Hey, I don't need hands anyway". I floated through this dimension for maybe ten minutes, and it really had me feel that this new dimension was one with our World. It was a pleasant experience, but had I never done any psychedelics before, I am certain it would have been very uncomfortable and scary. After coming down, I was a bit woozy for a few hours, not nauseous but just woozy.

After the appointment, my friend picked me up and drives me back to my Airbnb in Sedona, Arizona. As I arrived back to the house, I was still quite wobbly but decided some food may help me regain my senses. Just as I was about to cook something, my phone rang. It's my director, whom I have never met, and he is in town (I knew he was in Arizona but wasn't quite sure when we would meet up). It is 2:30 on a Monday, and I was on a scheduled day off. I had taken the ketamine around noon. He asked me to meet him and his wife for ice cream in 15 minutes. Shit. Being that he loves motorcycles and I live off mine, I have to get my head together and ride the moto down to the ice cream shop to meet him there.

I get geared up, grab Lambykins and go. I did ok driving, not great, but ok. I only had to make one U-turn. I am still feeling woozy, but I figure I'll be able to manage. As we sit outside eating ice cream, I have Lambykins on the table, and my director and I are chatting as Strawberry Fields comes over the radio. I began to stare off at the beautiful red rocks surrounding us all while trying to focus on the conversation. I am halfway between flowing with the music and talking with my director when he commented on how I speak very fast. Somehow, I quickly blame it on being from Boston and "We all talk fast up there". The meeting went pretty well overall (I think), outside a few stupid things I said (I'm sure I would have said them stone sober anyway). We took a few selfies that he sent to my manager. My manager knew I was off that day and knew what my appointment was, and said, "You met your director while high on ketamine, Michael?"

I didn't have much of a reply other than "Am I in a lot of trouble?"

Of course, I wasn't, but my workload did happen to increase a lot after that meeting. I believe I oversold myself on a lot of my abilities. Either way, the ketamine fully removed the seasonal depression from my life. Over the next two years, I would return to the same doctor maybe six or seven times, for "tune-ups" as I called them and a way to remain proactive with treating my seasonal depression.

LSD

Growing up, the first thing you think of when you hear LSD is someone taking it and going crazy on their roof with a bow and arrow and then jumping off and dying. As I dove more into psychedelics, and really anything important that mattered in life, I learned "the system" would demonize not only psychedelics, but anything that had you think outside the rigid confines of their nicely paved road. That's all well and good, but in doing so, that mindset really limits you from learning and your own growth through experimentation. This is about when I began to understand how ignorant our education system and the system in general was when I was growing up.

It was 2014, and I was (and still am) learning about psychedelics when a friend mailed me a puzzle box for Christmas. Of course, it took me a while to figure out how to open it, but when I did, there were four or five paper squares in there, and I knew instantly what it was. He had instructed me to try half of one and see how I did with it. At the time, I was going to sensory deprivation tanks, usually once a month and thought that would be a perfect time to ingest this new substance.

It was Friday afternoon, and I had wrapped up work and decided I would take half a tab of LSD as my friend recommended, as I jumped into a cab bound north to Fremont, a small artsy town just outside Seattle. When I arrived for my appointment, I think I started feeling it a little bit. The owner of the sensory deprivation tank studio told me that they were slow that day and I could stay in the tank for 2 hours instead of the normal one hour. This would be fantastic, I thought, especially with an extra hour. As I entered the tank, things seemed to feel a bit strange, not bad, just strange. Once in the tank, those feelings subsided, and I was more than relaxed over the next two hours with minimal differences from what I had felt before in these float tanks. I instantly thought the next time I tried this substance, I should consume one full tab.

Fast forward to 2017, as I was traveling the United States and living on my motorcycle. One of the stops where I planned to camp for a few days was in Grand Teton National Park. This was a park I was extremely fond of and one that was especially easy to camp on with a motorcycle, as it had a restaurant, laundry, and a full store walkable from your campsite. The park also had some trails I was familiar with that I thought may be a great place to take the full tab of LSD.

I awoke the next day and was beginning to think maybe this was not the right time to take it, and that a hike may be a better idea instead. As I walked to get breakfast and a much needed coffee, a black bear crossed the trail about 30 meters in front of me. Instantly, I wondered if that was bad luck like a black cat was. The bear wandered off into the thick shrubbery without incident, and I continued to the café, still yearning for a coffee to fully wake up.

Once my coffee arrived, I had decided a full breakfast was in order, as I had been eating a lot of Subway sandwiches since they packed nicely on the bike, and sometimes I would even ration the second half for a quick breakfast when packing up camp. My breakfast arrived, and it looked a hell of a lot better than the usual crushed semi-warm leftover Subway sandwich I was used to. I was still leaning towards a hike and reading some trail maps as I looked down at my breakfast plate. I instantly saw the calligraphy on one side of the plate with giant letters "LS" and on the other side of the plate another letter "D" (I still to this day don't know why those letters are on the dining ware in that park). That was it. I decided I would try the substance today!

Hiking back to my campsite I packed up some water, a few snacks, a tab of LSD, a notebook, pen, and my hammock and went out on a 1-mile hike to a quiet location where I could set up my hammock near a lake in the shade and watch the World through these new glasses to learn if I would gain a new insight.

I received a lot more than insight that day as the leaves, mountains, and lake all began to glow in a new shimmer that I had never seen before. I was set up about 2 meters inside the wood line. This location was perfect as hikers would walk by me and be very close to me, but wouldn't see me as they'd be looking out over the magnificent view towards the lake and not into the pine trees behind them. It wasn't just the feeling from the LSD, but I really felt as though I was invisible.

I stayed in that hammock on and off for the next several hours, and when the effects would slow down, I would make my way out to the beautiful lake and get a quick swim in before the effects came back to provide me with another wave of magic. During one of the more intense waves, I picked up my pen and notebook and just started writing. I had never written anything of substance before, and the notebook was really just in the event I thought of some task or something silly I needed to jot down. This time, I felt the notebook was a new tool I could use for communication, and I began scribbling in my already terrible penmanship (I'm left-handed). I wasn't thinking; just ideas were flowing out of me as the leaves were rustling, and a few squirrels chatted their approval of my ideas. Before I knew it, I had a solid outline of some type and felt it was time to put the pen away and return to the lake for a short swim.

I hadn't thought much about the writing for a few days, maybe even a week, when I needed to open the notebook to write out a "to do list" for my work week. It was then that I opened to the page from the previous week and thought all those scribblings sort of made a lot of sense, and was something I could try and use this writing in a positive manner.

It wasn't an hour later when I received an email from a global professional organization's magazine. They were looking for writers. I thought, Why not? It took me an hour or two, and with the help of a friend to proofread my work and fix a ton of grammatical errors, I then submitted the article. Not thinking anyone would take it seriously, and laughing at the article's origin, I just thought it would be a funny story someday.

A few weeks later, my email chimed, and it was the magazine asking me for formal permission to use the article and sign a release. I replied, allowing it and asked why there was so much formality around my name and why they required so much information. And that is how I ended up with my first article ever written being entered into the United States Library of Congress.

A Season of Change (Ayahuasca)

Having recently turned 50, and even though I feel it has been a super intense and successful ride (I'm still alive, so that's a barometer for success), I felt myself falling into a rut. I was unfulfilled with my job, and things were just… blah. I had even begun seeing a therapist to try and find a solution or the root cause of the rut I was in.

My job, although being a great vehicle in my life for college, certifications, and allowing me to travel the World, seemed to have broken down on the side of a desolate desert road and was spewing radiator fluid all over the cacti that surround it. My management and leaders above me were beyond spectacular, but I was just stuck and, having been there 21 years, felt it was time to put an end to this career. I requested and was granted a voluntary severance. My director had been providing many with the bad news of non-voluntary layoffs, and he didn't look too happy as he prepared me for the news over a video call. My reply was simply, "Sir, this will be the easiest call you have all day." I had a Cuban cigar and a glass of whiskey ready to partake in, once I heard the numbers. Instantly, I knew I had made the right decision as I felt a massive weight lifted off me.

What to do with my life now was the next question. It didn't take me too long to realize I should blast out on the BMW motorcycle and figure "it" out. While riding through Joshua Tree National Park, I reflected back to my time in Peru. I took a trip up the Amazon, and at a friend's suggestion, I tried this mystical hallucinogenic drink called ayahuasca under the guidance of a Peruvian shaman. It was an intense experience, to say the least and was (in my opinion) a solid restart of my entire system. I felt as though it was time to take this sacred drink again.

After a 3 month ride to British Columbia (nothing is ever a direct route for me) and experiencing some failures with the motorcycle, I arrived at my friend's retreat in rural Washington. Ayahuasca for me isn't a pleasant experience at all. It is a lot of work where you face your true inner self, even if you don't want to. This can be extremely painful and ugly without the ego and façade of the image you think you are. It is so intense that throughout my life, there are two things I have faced that scare me straight. Exiting an aircraft as a paratrooper with the 82nd Airborne Division and drinking ayahuasca. The rest is more or less manageable. You have no control over those, though. Fully handing the keys over to someone else isn't easy.

I was beyond nervous for this endeavor, so I thought prior to arriving, I would throw a few casts out to kill an hour or two. My first cast, I caught a beautiful bass. Now, the preparation for these ceremonies was not something to be taken lightly. This includes a very strict diet of no processed food, alcohol and meats limited to chicken and turkey, but fish was within the diet restrictions, so this would be a perfect meal to share with my new friends at the retreat.

I arrived on my BMW GS1200 and set up my tent where I would sleep after the ceremonies. 11 others would be drinking along with 2 practitioners overseeing the ceremony that would take place at 20:00 in a yurt on a beautiful piece of land next to a large river. It was the perfect setting and time for me to be in this place. I was beyond scared to drink this medicine again, but I trusted in my heart that it would provide me with some guidance in my life, as I was extremely ungrounded. Having taken this in Peru and at this location before, I felt confident in my decision. I was familiar with the effects it would have on me physically, emotionally, and spiritually. However, I didn't expect the impacts it would have on me this time.

I was about to consume ayahuasca for the 11th time in my life. The 12 of us gathered in the yurt around 19:30. Having participated in 10 ceremonies prior to the process felt natural and comfortable. That's not to say that I wasn't scared, but I was familiar with this beautiful plant, and most importantly, I trusted the plant and the people overseeing my consumption of it. In the past, the 1st night for me was not that painful and was more of a "getting to know you" feeling. Normally, it was a very pleasant experience, and I would see a lot of colors, and just the entire universe would unfold in front of me. The second night is when the effects of this medicine became serious and stepped up intensely.

This would not be the case tonight. Within 30 minutes of setting my intentions, consuming the brew and the singing of beautiful icaros (Native Peruvian songs) by the facilitators, I began to feel the effects of this plant medicine. About this time, the hallucinations began along with an uneasiness in my stomach. One of the side effects of drinking this medicine is that purging, or vomiting, is a frequent occurrence for many people.

What I am about to describe is my ayahuasca journey, so full disclosure, a lot of it won't make any sense whatsoever, but it is the outcome of the experience that I want to highlight. The hallucinations first came as a beautiful black panther crawling up my mat to sit in front of me. It was so close and real that I could feel the vibrations of it purring as we sat face to face for some time, just staring at each other. I thought this was a new form of an introduction. The muscular black panther disappeared after a short time, and at that moment of his departure, I was instantly thrust into the pits of a Hellish scene with a red sky and fire was everywhere. The only structures visible were totem poles made of fire screaming at me. Throughout my entire life, since I can remember, I had always thought that if things got too bad, I could. Well… Check out IE: suicide. For some odd reason, this comforted me. There was always that path of escape, so I rarely felt stuck. These thoughts were always lurking in the back of my mind. Not quite daily but frequently enough, and at times, I would use these feelings to motivate me to overcome difficult life situations we all face. This evening, instead of the getting to know you pleasantries that I expected, I was dragged into this hell of fear, forced, and I do mean forced to look at this, and as I am taking this all in, I heard a voice, "If you ever choose suicide, this will be your new home." I then began to violently throw up into a bucket (I had placed the bucket EXACTLY where I could find it in the dark). This went on for… well, until I learned my lesson.

After the ceremony, the host went by us, one by one, and checked in with all of us. I was still pretty shaken and putting the evening back together to try to ground myself. Upon formal closure of the ceremony, a group of us went inside the house to have tea and discuss our individual experiences. As I sat quietly in the corner of the room, listening to everyone's stories, and how they were all beautiful and gentle. I was still reliving the Hell I was shown; it would be a night of very little sleep for me. I think what really crushed me was that "plan B" was no longer a viable option. I was stuck with whatever happened in this life, and there was no "easy way out". You cannot imagine the impact of that reality settling inside of me. The next day, I was DONE. I was ready to leave and not stay for another ceremony. The day began with me crying inside my tent and really not much else. I talked with my friend who ran the retreat, sharing my feelings of wanting to leave. For me, even saying that I would quit is unheard of. But that first night was so painful that it was hard to imagine another two evenings of that. He shook it off as part of the growing experience. I knew he wasn't wrong.

Not being the smartest of people, the next night, not only did I attend the ceremony, but requested a 20% higher dose of the medicine. As I drank it, I said aloud, "Run towards the sound of guns," and tapped one of the practitioners and whispered to him, "Hey, please look out for me, I may need some help tonight." He promptly replied, "I've got you!"

I returned to my mat/astral spaceship with a full dose of ayahuasca in a cup that I was about to drink. This would be my 12th time consuming this magical potion from the jungles of South America. As I sat staring into the cup that would soon bring me into another world, I was as scared as I had ever been in my life, especially having just had one of the most frightening journeys of my life the night prior. Looking into the cup of dark molasses colored and textured fluid, I set my intentions and fearfully drank what was a little over 1oz, but this would prove to be more than enough to benefit from.

Similar to the prior evening, I sat back to let the medicine absorb into my body. There was nothing for me to do but let the medicine perform its work now. Once the singing of the icaros began, I could feel another entity coming towards me, but it wasn't the panther from the previous night, but a War of the Worlds type of jellyfish with tentacles. I was relaxed like in previous ceremonies, this was the hallucination I was used to. One of the tentacles came down, and at the end of it was the pattern of the inside of the ayahuasca vine, but I could tell it was an eye scoping me out. Yet again, I was eye-to-eye with a new entity introducing itself to me. What was constantly on my mind was if this entity would disappear and return me to the Hell I was in the previous night.

Pretty much as soon as the hopes of not returning to that Hell faded, yup, you guessed it, I returned to the exact same Hell as the previous night. Dammit! It was for a shorter period of time though (or so I thought, as time is relative in the spirit world). There were no voices or guidance this time though. So I wasn't quite sure of the lesson I was being taught, but I did vomit ferociously for quite some time. Once that began to wind down, my name was called, and I moved to the facilitator who would sing to me face-to-face. I was instantly uplifted and felt pure happiness. A happiness and peace with myself that I hadn't felt for years. I was comfortable within my own skin and felt as though I had been reborn and given a new chance to experience life through this new lens.

That evening, I went back into the room to have tea with everyone and was no longer huddled in the corner but was participating in the conversations. I also checked in on others to ensure none of them felt as I did the previous night. It was one of the best experiences I had to date with this medicine. I still had one more night to go through, so I was cautious not to become overly comfortable. It was time to rest, eat, hydrate and get my head together for tomorrow night's final ceremony.

I awoke in my tent still buzzing from the previous night's ceremony. A frequent side effect of ayahuasca is not being able to sleep. With little sleep, I was ready and excited to face the day with a renewed feeling of positive energy. I had not only made it through the ceremony but also came out the other side feeling confidence and happiness that I hadn't felt in years.

Even though I had this elated feeling, I was still cautious not to be too upbeat. I had a final ceremony that evening to go through, and I was certain there were still a few things I had yet to process. Hopefully, this evening would be where I would find the purpose that I originally came looking for, a star to steer by to light a path, even if it is just a few nearly dead chem lights to point the direction or a wind in a sail. Just something.

I passed the day by talking with the others and listening to their experiences, and just getting to know everyone a little better. As the day wore on, I began to feel uneasy yet again as to what that night's experience would be. With the ceremony starting at 19:30, the two hours leading up to it, I spent in solace and went fishing to pass the time (I had two solid bites but didn't set the hook, so off they went).

Upon entering the yurt, I sat on my mat and awaited being called on. Since this was the 3rd ceremony and I felt as though I had resolved a lot of what I had come for, I chose a smaller dose as I really wanted to be semi-coherent this night so that I could work with the plant, build a relationship, and have her assist me in bringing my purpose into the light.

As I returned to the mat with my cup of medicine, I sat looking deep into the cup for several minutes, asking for guidance before I drank the bitter tasting plant medicine. It didn't take too long before the muscular black panther appeared and strutted up the mat to be face-to-face with me, yet again. As I sat eye to eye with this magnificent beast, I noticed behind it was the entire universe filled with an infinite amount of lavender colored geometric fractal patterns. I felt so uplifted and began to repeat, "What is my purpose?" It was at this time that the panther left, and the universe melted into a dark, scary funhouse as I began to violently purge into my trusty bucket that was kept at my side. All the while, the facilitators were singing, and their icaros were resonating through my entire body. It was beyond overwhelming with every sense in my body was heightened as I was blasted with emotion from every direction.

One of my prouder accomplishments is being a paratrooper with the 82nd Airborne Division, anytime I have taken ayahuasca, my prior service to this great Country never crossed over during my hallucinations. As the madness of the funhouse carried on, I looked upward through the ceiling and could see an enormous 82nd Airborne insignia that lit up the entire universe. I once again was in a dark place and began asking why I was seeing this insignia. Did the plant have a problem with soldiers? paratroopers? Every time I asked, my surroundings just became darker and darker. Every so often, it would uplift me for a moment, where I would keep asking about the insignia. Each time I asked, I was thrust back into the funhouse of Hell. Obviously, I was asking the wrong questions (I learned this after the 3rd or 4th time of purging and visiting these dark places).

I am a slow learner. I managed to refocus for a moment, and it hit me. It was almost as if the plant was screaming at me and punishing me for not coming to the obvious conclusion of these signs. I had asked for the purpose during that ceremony, and that was it. The medicine was showing me what my purpose was. It is to help my fellow Veterans in some capacity (the conclusion I came to). This was what I had asked for, but I was just too overwhelmed by all the hallucinations to focus enough to obtain the answer that the plant was telling me.

While I am still very mindful of what lessons the plant medicine has taught me, life (as it tends to do) has had me distracted. I find myself backsliding into old habits and losing focus on my newfound purpose. I am now, however, alert enough to realize this and have the discipline to push myself back on track. As I continue to walk my path forward, I am thankful for having the resolve to attend and learn from this beautiful plant medicine. Although it is not a magic bullet. If you follow through on the lessons this plant teaches you, there is no doubt you will be a better person for yourself, those around you, and this world we all share.

Almost two years after attending these ceremonies, the lessons that the plant helped me acknowledge are still with me. The intensity does fade over time if you do not maintain the practice of integrating the lessons into your daily life. I did listen to the medicine's core message and took action on it, although with my travels, it hasn't been as deep as it should be. It took me a few months after the ceremonies to become grounded enough to where I felt comfortable taking action on the lessons that were provided to me.

After the ceremonies, I volunteered with a Veterans' assistance program. This program allows me to mentor Veterans transitioning into civilian life. Mentoring these young service members as they transition into a new world is an example of the fulfilment that the plant medicine was guiding me towards.

Overall, the ayahuasca experience was something that I felt was required for me to reset and realign myself. Ayahuasca is not a magic bullet. As with everything, you get out of it what you put into it.

Discipline is required for those lessons to stick with you and ensure you don't fall back into old, destructive habits. I am not one to recommend ayahuasca to anyone else; in fact, I usually caution against it, but it helped provide guidance immensely needed for my particular situation.

San Pedro (Huachuma)

In 2014, I was living in the Belltown area of Seattle, and like many, had obtained a medical marijuana card due to an injury sustained from serving in the United States Army. Say whatever you want. I had a medical card, and that is that. The card had to be renewed every year, which entailed going to see a "doctor" and stating your case. They would then provide a new card. The entire appointment took about 20 minutes, and you were cleared for the next 365 days. It was too easy, yet I found a way to complicate the hell out of a simple renewal process.

Rewind to 2012 in Cusco, Peru. I had heard about the San Pedro cactus from people in Iquitos, Peru, at my ayahuasca camp. Yet I never had the opportunity to experience it. In Cusco, however, it was easily available in the local market in a powder form and ready for consumption. San Pedro added color to my weekend hikes and adventures for the two months I stayed there. I found traveling throughout the mountainous country of Peru had a welcoming warmth and color to an already amazing environment. It was never something I went into too deeply. A teaspoon or two of this beautiful plant was something I had become quite familiar with and comfortable with. This power plant and I were building a solid relationship together, and I really enjoyed that.

Living in Seattle, it wasn't like you could obtain San Pedro at the Pike Place Market, but you could order it from the ever-trusting internet. It wasn't long before my Belltown apartment became a San Pedro processing plant. Over the next year, I learned through trial and error how to perfect the process for preparing this magical cactus. With my Friday afternoon medical marijuana appointment being the only thing on my calendar that day, I thought a solid spoonful or three to unwind from the week, re-center myself, and gain some clarity was in order. For the adventure today, I would be using a new San Pedro batch that I just freshly processed. I felt the seller ripped me off, as the cactus was much thinner than the previous ones. I would soon learn that wasn't the case.

Having the afternoon off from work for my appointment that was at 13:00 I packed up a day pack, consumed the cactus, and headed out on the 10 block walk to my doctor's office. The plant usually took about an hour before the effects were felt, and I knew by then I'd be in a park. This park overlooked Elliot Bay and the White Ghost known as Mt. Rainier. It was a perfect spot to relax, enjoy the sun, and just enjoy the presence of this plant.

None of this went as planned. As I arrived at the doctor's office, they informed me they overbooked and my appointment was pushed back until 15:00. With my license soon to expire and not wanting to rebook, I agreed I would return then, not remembering I was a psychedelic time bomb with the consumed San Pedro. I spent an hour wandering around Pike Place Market when I was reminded of the plant inside of me. Colors began shining much brighter, and I felt as if I was coming in and out of reality as I continued to walk through the bustling market.

By the time 15:00 rolled around, I was in the deepest San Pedro journey I had ever experienced. As I entered the doctor's office, which of course was plastered with all kinds of psychedelic posters and ornaments, I was having a difficult time speaking to her. What's worse is I couldn't hear her very well as that ever-familiar psychedelic static was kicking in, but this time it wasn't static but the roar of jet engines. It felt as though I was standing outside a jet turbine of a C-5 Galaxy. It was that loud. The doctor had to know I was on something or other, but didn't seem to care and renewed my license. I thanked her and quickly left before things got more intense.

It would be an interesting return walk to my apartment with nothing but that jet engine sound screaming. To add to the intensity, every curb I stepped off, it felt as though I was exiting an aircraft into a fractal psychedelic sky. I decided it was time to find a place of refuge, at least for a bit. I was very close to my favorite bar in Seattle, The 5 Point Café. This bar was usually quiet on a Friday afternoon. The bar had old TVs that would be playing Godzilla or Star Wars movies, and a jukebox that was usually blasting Metallica. Another reason I loved the bar is that in the men's bathroom above the urinal, there is a glass window. It's a periscope so you can see the Space Needle as you pee. I loved this place, the staff and bartenders loved me. This was the perfect location to decompress until the C-5 Jet engines dissipated in my head.

Within an hour of seeking refuge, I was composed enough for the short walk to return to my apartment. By this time, my head was too sideways to even attempt going to the park, and my couch would suffice as its replacement. The following day, I researched the different breeds of cacti and learned that the one I consumed was almost twice as potent as what I was accustomed. This explained the intensity I felt the day prior. All in all, it was a successful day. I had an adventure, learned about a new breed of San Pedro (the hard way), and most importantly, I renewed my marijuana license.

Although this story is meant to be humorous, there is one thing I realized as I wrote it. San Pedro is indeed a power plant, and how I was using it at the time was not how the medicine is to be used. This is not a social medicine that you would consume in a nonchalant way. It indeed is a powerful plant that deserves to be respected. In my own defense, I was very new to plant medicines at the time, but have matured with their use over the years and felt this message of respecting the plant needed to be stated.

Mushrooms (Psilocybin)

In October of 2025, I found myself on a boat in the Gulf of Thailand, about to perform my 40th scuba dive. I had been staying in a beachside hostel on the small island of Koh Tao. It is a popular place for divers, more for the lower prices than for the underwater wildlife. It was a good place to spend a couple of months, gain diving experience, and make new friends. I really grew to love the island and its lifestyle. This is when I overheard a dive master talking to someone about mushrooms and the great experience she had with them.

I was next to exit the ship with my semi-patented front flip into the warm ocean waters. It was time to embrace God's Aquarium, but I would be sure to seek out the dive master to learn more about these mushrooms upon resurfacing.

45 minutes later and back on the boat, I made my way towards the stern where the regular divers hung out for a smoke, a few whiffs off their yadom (a Thai herbal inhaler that is quite refreshing), and to locate the dive master. Once we started our conversation, I cut right to the chase, asking about where to obtain some mushrooms. She told me to go to the tattoo shop near my hostel and they would sell me some. We joked for a while about our psychedelic experiences and exchanged a few stories as the conversation flowed between that, traveling, and diving. I then thanked her as I suited up for my next dive.

Having a day off from diving, it would be a great time to swing by the tattoo shop and pick up these mushrooms. Purchasing them was a non-issue, just as easy as purchasing a Gatorade in a 7-11. There was a quiet local restaurant next door. This seemed like a good place to ingest these psychedelics. Once seated, I ordered some food, an iced cold Chang beer, and consumed 1 gram of mushrooms. I thought this small amount would suffice as I wanted to ease into this and not overdo it. By now, you realize the constant theme with any of my psychedelic stories seems to be "That didn't go as planned". Consuming that 1 gram of mushrooms in that Thai restaurant would soon prove no different.

It didn't take long before these little mushrooms hit me, hard and fast. I had barely finished my food, and the effects were coming on like a freight train. I rolled with it, knowing that this was just the beginning. The intensity continued to increase and was now at the point where it was extremely unpleasant. I had heard of these effects, known as a "bad trip", before, but never experienced this. Mentally, every thought that came into my head went to a worst case scenario and was just heavy. Inside my head, I was screaming, but my outer self was quite stoic. As the feelings continued to ramp up even more, I thought it best to pay my tab, return to my bed, and ground myself.

As I walked to the counter to pay, I noticed I had no cash. In Thailand, on these remote islands, it is common to only take cash and no credit cards. Lovely. The restaurant owner pointed out an ATM 1 block away. It may as well have been a mile for me in my current mental state. What's worse is when arriving at the ATM machine it was out of service. This is just great. I returned to the restaurant and, at this point, was not quite in a full panic but probably close. I explained the situation to the owner, who knew I had been here quite a while, and provided me a reprieve on paying until tomorrow.

Obstacle overcome, now to return to my bunk, and fast. As I entered the room, my bunkmate and fellow diver noticed I was "off". I quickly explained the story to him, and he had a good laugh. Once back in my bunk, my mind eased. I was happy I was in a place where I could wait these dark feelings out. It was at that moment when a new roommate arrived and wouldn't stop talking. To make matters worse, he was rambling about project management and corporate America jargon. He then moved to where he was sitting a foot from my bunk, facing me as his rambling continued. This sent me over the edge. I got up, and lightly grabbed him by the shoulders and said, "Son, I am having a bad mushroom trip. You really gotta go out for a bit". In which he respectfully did. All the while, my bunkmate was laughing.

It took a couple of hours of just relaxing before I came down enough to where I was able to communicate with the rest of the room. At this point, I was feeling a perfect buzz from the mushrooms and in very good spirits. The new roommate returned with some fresh dragon fruit, and we sat down and began talking (Non Corporate America talk). After a few minutes in what felt like mid-conversation, he went to his bunk and was focused on his phone.

When I asked him what he was doing, he stated he was stressed out as he needed to take his online scuba certification exam and wasn't confident he would pass. With me being extremely social at this time of the mushroom trip, I grabbed his phone and said, "I've got this". 5 minutes later, I tossed his phone back at him, "Congratulations, you are now scuba certified". He looked at the green approval screen on his cell phone with the score prominently visible, "100%".

The mushroom effects had finally begun to fade. My lesson from this was that even taking mushrooms in a semi-controlled environment, things can go sideways. I understand that the situation absolutely could have been darker so I refrained from consuming them the remainder of my stay in Thailand.

Scuba Stories

Scuba Certification

As I had begun to enter my 5th month of travel, not knowing where I would be sleeping the next night became routine. My mentality was "Future Mike will figure this one out, he always does." And I always did. That mindset isn't wrong, as crazy as it felt. However, as time pushed on and the countries began to be more in my rearview mirror, something was missing. It was a way to deeply experience a country, more than most might experience it. Similar to my past life with living off the BMW GS1200, it added a much needed color to my adventures. Most others were doing these adventures in a van or car. The BMW gave me that extra level of depth that awakened my senses and really allowed me to meet some wonderful people I wouldn't have otherwise.

Realizing I needed to experience something new (besides circling the globe solo), I needed something thrilling but something I had never done. I was two months into driving through Australia and about to board a flight from Sydney to Cairns. When I asked others in my hostel what was worth doing up there, one reply was always consistent: Scuba dive the Great Barrier Reef. That was it! I would become a certified scuba diver and head for the Great Barrier Reef.

I registered for the dates I would be in Northern Australia for a 5-day Open Water PADI Scuba Certification Class. This class would include two days of classroom/pool training and three days and two nights on a live aboard boat on the Great Barrier Reef. Upon filling out the school course paperwork, it seems that, due to my ripe old age of 51, I would require a physical. Not a big deal; there was a clinic across the street from my hostel. I am sure they would rubber stamp me through this, so I booked an appointment.

When I was called in to see the doctor, I noticed his clothing apparel seemed a bit…off. It wasn't until I went into his exam room that I noticed posters of Elvis all over the walls. Now his butterfly collar, gold glasses, and slicked back hair made sense. He was an Elvis impersonator, or at least a big fan. Once reviewing the physical requirements with him, he explained the physical entailed much more than I expected, including chest x-rays, hearing tests, vision tests, drug tests, etc.

So I am not saying I cheated on this physical, nor am I disclosing if I did, but how I would complete such an act. What I am saying is I passed the physical with flying colors. Sweet. I sent the paperwork off to the diving school and was formally accepted into the program. I was still smiling as I boarded my flight from Sydney to Cairns in Australia (this was one of the northernmost points of this mind blowing continent).

Arriving on time to class (15 minutes prior to its scheduled start), I learned the class would be small. Myself, a young man from France, and an American female from San Diego. Our instructor was from

Pittsburgh. Normally, I would hold that against her, but she was beyond stunning, so it was easy to let that go. Class instruction on the equipment, different emergency protocols, hand signals, and a tutorial of almost any underwater emergency we could possibly encounter. This was the first half of the day. After lunch, it was time to put these lessons to use, using our scuba gear in an enclosed 12-foot deep pool.

The first thing in the pool we performed, even before learning about our gear, was a swim test. This consisted of treading water for 10 minutes in place and a 300 meter swim. Upon successfully passing this, it was time to learn about all our gear. This included the air tank, BCD, respirator, fins, mask and snorkel, and how to successfully connect them all together.

It was now time to put on the scuba gear and go underwater in the pool for the first time. I will admit this caused a bit of anxiety for the first few minutes, even though we were just a few feet under. It was a new experience for me and the others, so that was normal. In no time, we were nailing the different drills, such as mask removal and replacement while under the water and buoyancy control. We also performed drills in the event we ran out of air, how to signal and use your buddy's secondary air supply (I, of course, made sure I was paired with the instructor). Little did I know at the time, but paying attention to this lesson would prove to be lifesaving in just a few weeks in Indonesia.

After successfully completing the classroom, pool sessions and passing a written exam, we were ready to take our skills into the ocean. The next day, we were scheduled to meet at 0700 at the boat launch, where we would be on a live aboard boat for the next three days. The remainder of our training and honing our skills would be performed in the open waters of the Great Barrier Reef in Australia. This is where we would hopefully pass and become Open Water Certified Divers. Bad ass!

It was 07:00, and the location was a pier in Cairns, Australia, as 30 of us were boarding a live aboard boat to perform 9 scuba dives over the next 3 days and 2 nights. There were only 3 of us who had never performed an open water scuba dive before, and I was one of them. It would take 5 dives while completing our drills for us to obtain our PADI open water certification. We were ready.

It took the boat about 3 hours to get out to the reef for our first dive. 27 of the others were seasoned divers. As the newbies, we felt privileged that they'd help us gear up and make jokes about our fumbling around prior to getting into the water.

Others may disagree with me, and that is fine, but I have skydived and to me, nothing felt closer to jumping out of an airplane as a paratrooper than scuba diving. You suit up, perform checks on your gear and your scuba buddy's gear, shuffle to the edge of the boat, give an OK to the dive master who checks your air is on (I always stuck my hand out and yelled "ALL OK JUMPMASTER!" just to get into the moment a bit more), and jump off the boat into the water. I understand the two experiences are almost polar opposites, but what isn't is the comradery and the procedures prior to diving (or jumping out of an airplane).

As soon as I hit the ocean waters of the Great Barrier Reef in full scuba gear, I felt two things: A brief moment of anxiety, just as I felt in the pool during onshore training, and when we signaled to go down.

This was a moment of bliss and freedom as you leave the world you know and enter a realm of tranquility beneath the ocean. It was so similar to exiting an aircraft, as you leave the chaos and perform the 4 second count prior to your parachute opening. Both are moments when you have a quick chat with the Big Guy upstairs and are alone in the world. There are few experiences in life that compare to these. I was instantly hooked on scuba diving.

Our first five dives were work. They encompassed the same drills over and over that we performed in the pool. The objective was to review the same emergency procedures for a multitude of issues that you can face while underwater and how to calmly overcome them. This was another similarity to being a paratrooper. The only big difference is that there was less yelling for your mistakes, but the instructor did have a whiteboard to correct any errors you were making while on the dive. Another reason I knew my instructor was great was when she wrote my mistakes on her whiteboard, for I literally could hear her stern voice in my head just as clear and loud as if we were above water.

Upon all three of us successfully meeting the criteria, we were now PADI Certified Open Water Scuba Divers. Now it was time to begin having fun and enjoying the benefits of diving. We were on the Great Barrier Reef after all, and the coral and wildlife we saw over the next 3 days were magical. We were literally in God's aquarium. Each of the dive sites we experienced had something unique to offer, from schools of colorful fish to sea turtles, to even a couple of nurse sharks and reef sharks. If I wasn't hooked before with this new hobby, I surely was now.

The remainder of the days were passed with dives, delicious food and wonderful new friends. The beauty of this live aboard boat was absolutely the people who surrounded me. We each had different experience levels in diving and were from countries all around the world, yet we all bonded over this one passion, scuba diving. Once the evening festivities died down, instead of returning to the tight quarters below deck, a few of us decided to sleep on the open upper deck of the vessel. This was the perfect way to wind down. We would tell a few jokes while staring at the Southern Cross as it slowly made its way across the sky until we fell asleep. In the morning, we awakened to the sunrise hitting this spectacular part of the world and lighting up the Australian Flag. A feeling of accomplishment washed across me each day and evening of this trip. It may have been the most rewarding time along my travels so far with good reason. I had found a new way to add even further adventure to my travels.

Indonesia

My visa was nearing expiration in Australia (I had spent almost 90 days in country), and my speeding tickets were exceeding $1700 Australian. The speeding tickets were from cameras. In the United States, the Constitution protects us (you can fight and win those tickets 100% of the time in the USA, but not in Australia). It was time to choose a new country to visit, at least for a short while. To me, it made sense to leave my beloved Oceania and head north. Looking at the map, Southeast Asia beckoned.

Indonesia, in particular, seemed to be the best choice, and it would be my next destination. Bali, to be exact. This would provide a less westernized culture than the previous countries I had visited. Another advantage was that it appealed to my new interest. I kept hearing how magnificent the scuba diving was there. So that new passion would now be incorporated into my adventures.

After the whirlwind trip through Australia, the first three days in Bali (except for some morning surfing) were spent resting in my hotel room. I needed the time to recharge and just sit back and pretend I was on vacation. Yes, I know I am sort of always on vacation, but even with this laid back lifestyle, the constant moving becomes a full-time job.

Once rested, it was time to book several ferries and boats out to Komodo National Park. It isn't easy to reach. Visiting this epic National Park would provide me with the chance to see Komodo dragons, the largest lizard on Earth. There would be plenty of opportunities to hone my new skills as a diver. This was an experience I could not miss while visiting Indonesia.

The day trip to Komodo Island was fantastic. What made it most memorable was actually seeing a few of these giant reptiles in the wild, up close and personal as I was comfortable with. That distance happened to be about 6 feet for me. Our tour group was instructed to let this monster through as the giant reptile chose the direction it wanted to travel in, and it moved with a purpose!

These giants can move up to 12 miles per hour. Some weigh as much as 150 pounds. They can take down local deer, and they have no natural enemies. This meant we were guests on their island, and without a stick or other type of weapon, we were not on the top of the food chain. It's always a humbling moment when you realize this.

After a day exploring Komodo National Park with large sticks in hand, I found myself in Flores, Indonesia. It's a small island about an hour's boat ride from Komodo National Park. Little did I realize how much of a scuba diving mecca this was. There were literally dive shops and tours every 3 or 4 buildings. It was densely populated with the scuba community. It was perfect. This would be a great home base for a week or so to dive and continue catching up on rest from the Australia travels. It was now time to book a scuba adventure in Bali, Indonesia.

It took about a week to get to Flores, Indonesia, from Bali, as it is over 1,000 kilometers away. This was accomplished via three ferries and finally, a 4 day cruise. The cruise was a blast, but once aboard, I realized it was a one-way cruise and I would have to find a ferry back (that could take up to 36 hours) or book a return flight to Bali. Normally, this would alarm most people, but I had time to kill and quickly learned Flores was an Indonesian scuba diving mecca. Some of the most beautiful underwater wildlife could be seen diving here. This was not a bad place to have a several-day layover.

It didn't take long to find a scuba tour company. It had only been a few days since my prior dive, and I was already itching to get back underwater. I chose a dive center based on its 3 dives in one day regimen. Most of the other dive centers only offered two dives in one day. This would help rack up my dive numbers (and my experience, as I would soon learn).

Diving the Komodo Islands is just amazing on so many levels. The biggest draw is the wildlife. The second draw is the strength of the underwater currents. On an average dive, we would float with the current for close to an hour and travel several kilometers during the dive. The current was a constant underwater river that was at times overwhelming, depending on the direction it was taking you.

If you got caught in a side current, it would feel like you were on the Space Station and someone just cut your tether and you were floating off into nothingness. Feelings of anxiety emerged when this happened, and this caused me to go through more of my air and shorten my dive. It was always important to remain calm, move slowly, and not overreact. That's easier said than done.

The cool part about these currents is that when I was in a "controlled" area, I could just watch the beautiful corals go by. The downside was that if I saw a turtle or another cool species, I really couldn't get to it as I was swept along with the current. We were told, if possible, to get low to the ocean floor and grab a large rock as an anchor so we could enjoy the wildlife.

I took this rock grabbing suggestion as I happened upon three beautiful manta rays. They were huge, about 12 feet in width. While blowing by them in the current, it was like they were in an underwater thermal, hovering in place motionless, unaffected by the strong currents. It was like watching a stealth fighter jet hover. Meanwhile, I was doing my best to slow down to try to remain close to them. As I descended to the ocean floor seeking refuge from the currents behind a large piece of coral, I grabbed a rock. I instantly felt something sharp on my fingers. I had accidentally grabbed a sea urchin, and the spines were in all my fingers including deep under my fingernails. The next instant a large gushing of green fluid began pouring out of my fingers. This is when I learned you bleed green as I was deep enough underwater that colors would change, and it looked like I had been rolling around in some saguaro cactus or been on the losing side of a fight with a porcupine. I had spines sticking out from every part of my wetsuit.

Realizing there was nothing I could do about the bleeding until I surfaced, my focus was on watching the manta rays flying by as the current pulled me just underneath them. During this time, I religiously checked my air levels on my respirator. Once I hit 60 bar (25%), it would be time to slowly return to the surface.

We began our ascent to a 3 minute safety stop at 5 meters below the surface to allow our bodies to adjust to the pressure. At around 10 meters and still being abused by the strong currents, I went to breathe in, and there was nothing there. It was as though I was breathing through a straw, and then suddenly someone put their finger over the end. I was out of air. This was a good time to see how much of the training I actually retained and how much I ignored while being distracted by the beautiful scuba instructor in Australia.

This was part of the adventure and part of learning. What I didn't expect was that upon our ascent, my air ran out, even though moments earlier I had checked and confirmed I was at about 25%. This was another "So this is how it ends" moment. There wasn't much time to think about that, as I was not prepared for running out of air. I figured I just had moments before I would black out due to no oxygen.

Being about 10 meters deep, I knew I could have just surfaced quickly to get air and many people probably would have done that. Just as in jumping out of airplanes, you train for these types of scenarios. Also, the approach is to take your time, as you have the rest of your life to resolve the no air issues, just as you would with a parachute malfunction. The problem with that mindset is that the end of your life is only seconds away.

Fortunately, my dive partner was only a short swim away. I swam over to him as quickly as possible, signaled him I had no air, and calmly (I was actually panicking at this point) grabbed his secondary air hose and took a much needed breath in.

That first breath in was a relief on every level you can possibly imagine. We then performed our 3 minute safety stop by using both of his air supplies before we surfaced. Even with my fingers still bleeding from the sea urchin spines and having run out of air, I managed to make a couple of jokes as we swam back to the safety of the boat. This is where we learned that my regulator was faulty and provided a false reading on my air remaining. That was a bit of a relief that it wasn't some rookie mistake by me.

The joking ended on my next dive that day. As soon as I hit the water, I had some massive anxiety about the no air issues and going under. It was so intense with everyone on the team already submerged, I was just sitting there on the surface fearing to let the air out of my BCD to sink and join the rest.

After a few moments, it passed, and I joined them. I don't think I have ever swam as close to a dive partner as I did on that dive. My air barely lasted 32 minutes as my stress and anxiety were causing me to breathe faster, using up my air rather quickly. This was fine with me, as I really had no interest in staying underwater.

Once back on the boat, I was seriously thinking that scuba diving wasn't for me and would bow out of it using one excuse or another. The lack of air experience was so traumatizing. I began to think back to the Army and our jumps. Whenever someone had a bad jump, the best way to overcome it was to put them on the very next jump to regain their confidence so they could continue to be effective. Since diving and jumping had so many parallels, I thought this would be the best way. I booked three more dives the next day with the mindset that if I didn't overcome it, I would quit diving. I owed it to myself to give it one more try.

It was a relief to be back on the boat and done diving for the day. My anxiety level was still pretty high, having run out of air 10 meters below the ocean's surface on my second dive. Nonetheless, I registered to dive the following day. There was a sense of relief knowing that I would have the same diving partner. He understood the emotions going through my head, and he would be right at my side to help me through the next dive.

The remainder of the boat ride back to the dock consisted of me pulling sea urchin spines out from everywhere on my body with needle-nosed pliers. That's one way to pass the time. The spines under my fingernail would need to be pulled out by a doctor at a medical clinic somewhere in Flores. My biggest concern was that it might become infected. The closest clinic was a few kilometers outside of town, so I would have to taxi to get there.

Then, upon disembarking from the boat, I looked up and saw an Indonesian Naval Base. Right behind the gate was a giant red cross. I decided to give it a try, not expecting any success. The Military Police stopped me instantly, asking what I was doing. I showed them my finger and pointed to the red cross behind them. They invited me in, and within 5 minutes, I had an Indonesian Naval Officer using a razor blade to pull the pines out from under my fingernail. After about 45 minutes of him carefully removing all the spines, he gave me some antibiotics, he only charged me about $12 (US), and sent me on my way. During the whole ordeal, he and I were chatting quite a bit over our past military experience, and we even exchanged phone numbers. We trade texts every few weeks.

With the sea urchin spines removed, the next day came, and it was time to get over my anxiety from the previous dive. The first dive of the day proved to be challenging, and my only motivation was to just survive it. I wasn't too concerned with the enjoyment or the wildlife. Fortunately, by the second dive, I had regained my confidence and was back to enjoying this hobby again. Swimming by seven manta rays changed my mind and helped me reprioritize my goals.

My 30-day Indonesian visa was nearing expiration. Indonesia has around 7,000 islands and was much too large to cover in 30 days. Even having experienced 10 of the islands felt rushed. I knew I would need to slow my travel to more deeply absorb these countries. Having done SCUBA dives in two countries, racking up 19 dives, and overcoming adversity provided renewed confidence. I was ready for the next country: Thailand.

Koh Tao, Thailand

Having a new addiction to scuba diving, it didn't take me long to learn that Koh Tao (an island in southern Thailand) was another mecca for my new hobby of scuba diving. Koh Tao wasn't a very large island, and I was a bit concerned I would succumb to island fever. The big difference is now I would be spending much of my time underwater, thus making the island much larger and more exciting than the previous visited islands I had visited. This new hobby opened up a new world to me, similarly to learning to off-road on the BMW GS1200. They both were previously unexplored frontiers that drew me in and begged for more exploration after each experience.

Koh Tao isn't exactly easy to travel to from anywhere, as you need to fly or bus, and then take a 3 hour ferry out to the island. This, to me, made it a great destination as I knew those who were there were far off the beaten path and would be well grounded (mentally, not geographically). Although the island was touristy, it was small enough that it was easy to make friends quickly. Another draw to this isolated location was that almost anyone who was here long-term had the same line, "I came here to visit for two weeks and never left, and that was X years ago." This clearly told me it was a great place to set up a home base for a while and improve my diving skills.

Outside of a short blast up to Cambodia and some rest time in Bangkok (yes, it is possible to rest in Bangkok), I spent the next month in scuba classes for advanced and rescue diver certifications. I spent my days filled with fun dives, time on the beach, and just taking a few moments to enjoy chatting with someone at a bar while being fully present in life. The laid back island vibe and hospitality were something that had been missing in my previous travels, due to my constant moving. Koh Tao is where I was learning to finally slow down and really embrace the moment without tripping myself up with previous racing thoughts of "what's next?" This provided an important step into my new lifestyle.

The happiness of being in the moment with my focus on watching my dive log fatten and my circle of friends grow is all I need at this time. I wrapped up my updates while sitting at a beach bar with a cold Chang beer. It had me thinking that one day I may tell others, "Yeah, I just came here for two weeks, but that was X years ago."

Rescue Diver Certification

There are several requirements prior to beginning the rescue diver course. One has an advanced scuba certification. This certification allows you to dive to a depth of 30 meters and further educates you on proper buoyancy while underwater.  Having just taken this a month prior helped me, as the fundamentals were still fresh in my head. The second was to obtain an updated First Responder course. This part of the class was half a day and entailed covering CPR, proper bandage application, and procedures on how to help others in numerous types of emergency situations, from car accidents to everyday incidents you may come across. Once that was completed and I passed the online course, the real challenge began. Scuba rescue operations while at sea include incidents deep below the water's surface.

The water rescue portion was what I was really itching to learn. It was a challenging experience both mentally and physically. Many of the scenarios involved how to identify and treat divers who are exhausted, panicked, or unconscious. Another major prop I will give Scuba Shack is that the actors in these scenarios did a fabulous job (I think I may still have a lump on my head from rescuing the panicked diver). Most work was in rescuing an unconscious diver underwater. This included how to bring them safely to the surface, how to bring them to the boat while they are yelling for help and providing rescue breaths every 5 seconds (including performing this work while taking both your gear and their gear off). It was humbling how much work and focus it took to perform these tasks with precision. My partner and I managed to successfully perform these tasks both solo and as a team.

Upon completing our final skills test (that was an underwater navigation search and rescue), we both relaxed on the boat, celebrating with some coffee and fresh fruit, when we heard several people screaming for help in the water. It was the final exam. My partner and I had to rescue three divers needing help. We had to prioritize each one and work as a team to safely rescue them all in order of priority. We performed this successfully.

We both passed our course, and our confidence and diving abilities greatly increased from attending this class

I want to thank all the wonderful people at Scuba Shack and our instructor, Sita, for the great experiences during this class and for our fun dives we frequently performed.

Dos Ojos Cavern Dive – Mexico

My main purpose of traveling to Mexico was tacos, but diving was a close runner-up as a reason to visit this incredible country again. Diving over the past six months has almost replaced my addiction to motorcycling, making it yet another bad decision as a hobby choice.

I was on the Yucatan Peninsula in Mexico, and much of this land was created from a giant asteroid. That would be THE giant asteroid that created the Ice Age and killed off the dinosaurs. With this massive disruption in this area, the ocean floor was lifted in a strange way that created cenotes. These essentially are old caves that are now flooded with fresh water. There are about 5,000 of these cenotes throughout the Yucatan Peninsula and they are quite magical. Having to mark my checklist off (I'm making this list up as I go, by the way, as a month ago I couldn't tell you what a cenote was), scuba diving in one of these seemed like it would be incredible, and it was. Sorta.

In Thailand, I had done a swim through one or two times on occasion. Not even caves or caverns, but about 20 meters. It wasn't something I ever enjoyed, but it wasn't the worst experience either. I wasn't quite sure how I would feel during a 52 minute, ¼ mile dive through my first cenote. Upon arriving and seeing the other divers in the crystal clear water with the sunlight mysteriously peering through the overgrowth of old forest above the cave, I was instantly put into a state of awe based on how beautiful it was. After donning our scuba gear and jumping into the cenote, the cool water was quite refreshing from the heat and humidity in the jungle above us. After a few minutes of joking around and performing a buoyancy test, we were ready to begin exploring this cenote underwater.

It didn't take long before the beautiful, glowing natural light was absorbed by darkness. We had nothing but our small flashlights and a string along the bottom to guide us for the next hour. As we swam along, there were stalagmites and stalactites on either side of us. Some were so old they had formed natural columns in the still, crystal clear and dark water we were slowly navigating through.

We were about 30 minutes or so into the dive when I noticed my heart began beating quite rapidly. It was beating at a rather uncomfortable rate. I tried to shake it off, as mentally I felt great, but it seemed to worsen. With my heart now beating faster, my breathing also began to increase. I knew I had plenty of air, as I am religious about checking my oxygen levels. I did what I could to dismiss it, but my mind wouldn't allow me to shake it off.

With all this going on, I began to float to the surface. Normally, this would just be frustrating, and I would have to close my eyes, exhale, and sink back to the level I wanted. The issue now is that there was no surface. There was only the cavern ceiling. If I hit the cavern roof, I would probably hit my head and it would possibly be a "lights out" situation. I did not want this. We were in a semi-single-file line, although I was a bit more elevated than the others, in several ways now that I think about it. There really was nothing or no one I could reach out to for help. What were they going to do? Give me a hug? I was on my own here, and as with previous situations, I had the rest of my life to determine how to resolve this mess and get my head, and more importantly, my body under control.

It took a couple of minutes to do just that. A short while later, I was enjoying the cave, being super calm and relaxed. It felt like coming out of an intense psychedelic trip and realizing that you are on the other side of it (and a stronger person for having undergone the experience). Then, it happened again. Not quite as intense but enough for me to mentally note that this sort of diving wasn't for me, or at least it wasn't for me at that particular time.

As we neared the entrance of the cavern from where we started, I saw the shimmering neon green light of the sun through the water and began seeing the other divers floating gently above me. This was a welcome and beautiful sight. My first cavern dive had been logged, and as I surfaced, I looked at my new friends around me and simply said, "Well, that was quite a trip". At that moment I decided I am long overdue for a couple of cold Tecates and some much needed tacos to help my mind and body regroup.

Epilogue

It is September 2025, and as I wander Southeast Asia, I reflect on this piece of art I just submitted for the world to review. Even with the humor and adventures contained within the pages of this book, it's important to realize that 8 years of growth and challenging the status quo were also required to create it. With my personal development, there have been numerous setbacks, as growth doesn't always happen in a linear progression. Life will always throw obstacles your way and it is your duty in finding ways to overcome them.

The greatest takeaways from my experiences are that much of my successes come from accountability and discipline from within myself. The ability to fully accept responsibility when mistakes or poor decisions were made and accept ownership of them. Accountability comes to the forefront of your life when there is only you. There is no way to blame a coworker, friend, or family member for the situation you've gotten yourself into (although Lambykins has fallen on his sword for me on more than one occasion). Without accepting and learning from your mistakes, reaching your full potential is impossible, much less succeeding in the fast-paced, stressful environments I choose to reside in.

Discipline is another core fundamental I rely on throughout these stories. When I was traveling abroad, there were no missed calls or deadlines. If the power went out in Nicaragua, I was walking with my laptop 3 miles (uphill both ways) to a coffee shop where I could complete my assigned tasks, so it was seamless to others as to my location. Upon returning to the United States, it frustrated me that when this happened to my coworkers in their homes, they took no action other than to send the team a text message and to wait out the power outage. The stories are always romanticized when you're working remotely, but the inner workings that went on behind the scenes never stopped, at least for me. It wasn't easy to remain invisible for almost eight years, but maintaining that discipline was mandatory for my success during that time.

Having left Corporate American life over 2 years ago, I completed my long-term goal of "getting off the wheel." Although traveling, volunteer work, and new hobbies occupy my time, there will come a point where I will require a deeper fulfillment. I am confident in my abilities to recognize when this time arrives; with it, more adventure stories will surely follow, and who knows, maybe a second book.

About the Author

Michael Huber, from Augusta, Maine, is a traveler, motorcyclist, scuba diver, psychedelic explorer, and writer with six continents under his belt. In his former life, he was a paratrooper with the 82nd Airborne Division. That high-intensity lifestyle prepared him for his current life as a moto vagabond, where over the past eight years, Michael has been embracing adventure on his BMW R1200GS and  backpacking the world. He has no intention of returning to a "normal life." Michael is currently based in Southeast Asia.

Biography

Michael Huber-Was raised in the State of Maine in the United States of America, and began his life adventure by joining the United States Army after barely graduating high school at the bottom of his class. Once in the Army, he volunteered to be a paratrooper with the 82nd Airborne Division. After 5 years of military service, Michael took his skills and entered corporate America as a project manager. He then became a leader within the project management field for 15 years. He accomplished this while simultaneously attending Boston University, from which he graduated with a bachelor's degree in Business Management.

Since 2017, Michael has been a world traveler and, for 6 years, lived off his motorcycle while continuing to excel in his professional career. Michael left his position as a senior project manager in 2023 and has since traveled the world pursuing adventures and building unique and lasting relationships along his travels. Michael is a leader, a seeker, and an explorer. His creative methodology has propelled him into a position where he currently mentors Veterans transitioning out of the military and into corporate life as he continues his World travels.

www.ingramcontent.com/pod-product-compliance
Lightning Source LLC
Chambersburg PA
CBHW061216070526
44584CB00029B/3859